"Dr. Dan and I have worked together on a variety of projects, so I know firsthand how his strategies and techniques can assure success in business, sports, and security work."

—Anthony Poveromo, president, 21st Century Security

"Dr. Dan Schaefer's strategies give me an entirely different approach to challenging situations. They allow me to step back and see things from a broader perspective, and that's how opportunities are found."

—Will Rico, CEO, Commonmind

"Dan helps guide your actions strategically with forethought toward more thoughtful business and life decisions."

—Bernard Ascher, president, the Navigators

"Dr. Dan helped me tap the lessons of my past to build confidence today about success in the future."

—David North, broadcaster; president, David North Media

"Dr. Schaefer and his approach have brought my golf game back to a level I didn't think I was going to revisit. I have done a great deal of work in this field in the past, and Doc's approach makes a lot of sense and is extremely useful in my game. I can't wait to have him work with some of my students next year."

—Jim Weiss, head golf professional, Cold Spring Country Club; former course record holder at Bethpage Black (65)

"Dan is an executive strategist, performance coach, and confidential sounding board who often flies below the radar. He likes to say he sells mistakes. As someone who works with executives at the highest levels, Dr. Dan knows a thing or two about how they think—and how to get their attention."

—Fred Klein, cofounder, Gotham City Networking, Inc. and Fredslist

"I highly recommend and endorse Dr. Schaefer's mind game techniques for enhancing athletic and business performance."

—Richard G. Gertler, senior partner, Thaler & Gertler, Attorneys at Law

"The genius of Dr. Schaefer is that his peak performance strategies are simple to understand but incredibly effective. There is no silly rah-rah fluff, only actual, tested, and proven strategies. We urge all of the families we coach to pay close attention to everything he says."

—Andrew Lockwood, JD, and Ken Schreiber, publishers, StudentAthleteMagazine.com

"I began to use Dr. Dan Schaefer as my mind-strategy specialist in August 2002. Dr. Dan brought to the table a plethora of mind strategies I use quite regularly in my athletics, in my business, and at home with my children."

—Jody-Lynn Reicher, MMA fighter; ultrarunner; owner of Fine Tuning Therapy, Inc.

"[Dr. Dan's] concept of 'every decision you make both on and off the field becomes a business decision' helped me control the chaos in my life… I now have the mindset to be a strong leader and to lead my company in the direction it needs to be steered. Because of Dr. Dan, I have created a six-figure business and delivered my message to thousands of people both in the gym and onstage… I have Dr. Dan to thank for leading me in the right direction and teaching me the tools and strategies to take my life to the next level."

—Rahsheen Slaughter, strategic health coach; owner, Meta-Burn Fat Loss Studio; creator of the 28 Day Belly Fat Diet

"While working with Dr. Dan I discovered tools that have propelled me from being a behind-the-scenes producer to hosting and executive producing a television show broadcast from the number-one market in the country. His teachings helped me discover and facilitate expressing my ultimate potential, and his work continues to help me during my ever-evolving journey of fulfillment and satisfaction… The competitive edge he speaks about truly exists and it is obtainable by following his practical advice."

—Donna Drake, president, Drake Media Network, Inc.; host and executive producer, *Live It Up!*

"In Dan Schaefer's *CLICK!*, you'll discover a systematic approach that'll enable you to make better decisions and achieve better outcomes... You'll learn to turn off the noise and focus on what's important in any situation... Within just minutes you can dramatically increase your ability to concentrate, improve your attitude, boost your confidence, and see more clearly."
—Victor Urbach, president, Altegent LLC;
publisher, The Urbach Letter (www.UrbachLetter.com)

"The concept of negative self-talk alone makes this book a must-read!"
—Robert Levin, chief executive officer and publisher,
The New York Enterprise Report

"Dr. Dan's *CLICK!* system has given me an expanded perspective for myself and very powerful tools to offer clients. Dr. Dan recently placed a client of mine in a very high-level internship and presented his YOU, Inc. strategy at a high school with 6,000 students."
—Renee Brown, career consultant and CEO,
Your Career My Advice

"When I met Dan, I was insecure and not clear on how to approach business decisions with confidence. I needed to connect my business brain with my musical soul but I did not have the supplemental knowledge. Soon after a few long talks with Dan, I was able to organize my ideas and learn how to simplify the developing process of creative business. It changed my life."
—Pancho Tomaselli, bass player for War and Film

"Dr. Dan Schaefer is quite good at showing you how to get an edge and maintain mental focus. *CLICK!* is the playbook for successfully and efficiently removing obstacles and immersing yourself in an atmosphere that will positively impact your career."
—Bryan R. Adams, cofounder, FAB Communications;
entertainment publicist

"Dr. Dan Schaefer gives you practical life applications that are attainable by following his system. *CLICK!* will show you how to control negative thoughts and how to communicate in a more effective way. I encourage anyone who's committed to making positive changes in his or her life to read this book today and start living life to the fullest."

—**Corey Louchiey, president, NFLPA NY/NJ;**
retired NFL offensive tackle
(Buffalo Bills and Atlanta Falcons)

"Who doesn't believe that businesspeople, like athletes, require ongoing coaching and training in order to perform at maximum effectiveness? Dr. Dan bridges these worlds exquisitely and marries multiple disciplines while delivering his knowledge and advice in a real-speak manner. As a consultant and trainer myself, Dan is always at the top of mind when I meet with executives who would be receptive to his programs."

—**Adrian Miller, president, Adrian Miller Sales Training;**
founder, Adrian's Network

"In representing both active NHL players and the most promising prospects, I want to provide my clients with unique strategies to improve their personal performance on and off the ice. Dr. Dan has been a valuable resource. His *CLICK!* system is a perfect fit."

—**Lloyd M. Friedland, Esq.,**
Librett, Friedland & Lieberman, LLP

"Dr. Dan has taken my way of thinking to a level of complete control when it comes to sports performance. Now, when I'm out on the course, I represent all my company is. I am so driven with every race I do thanks to the trust Dr. Dan has taught me to have in myself."

—**Louise Senato, triathlete**

CLICK!
The Competitive Edge™
for Business, Sports, and Entertainment

To
LEN

WIN!!!.
when Losing is not A option

Best Wishes,
Dan

For more information:
dan@danschaeferphd.com
www.DanSchaeferphd.com

Book design by:
Arbor Books, Inc.
www.arborbooks.com

Printed in the United States of America

CLICK! The Competitive Edge™ for Business Sports & Entertainment
Dan Schaefer PhD

1. Title 2. Author 3. Self Help/Motivational

Library of Congress Control Number: 2010936648

ISBN 13: 978-0-615-40339-7

CLICK!

The Competitive Edge™

for Business, Sports, and Entertainment

Dan Schaefer, PhD

Peak Performance Strategies® LLC

*Dedicated to
Barrie Sue—
She is my
spirit,
white light,
and
Love*

TABLE OF CONTENTS

Foreword by Chad Pennington xvii

Preface by David Peretz, MD xix

Acknowledgments xxi

Introduction: The Toolbox xiii
    Mind Game Strategies xxix
    Business Performance Strategies xxix
    Owners Manual xxx

Chapter 1: The Wish List 1
    The Wish List 3
    The Key to the Wish List 5
    What Now? 9
    Toolbox Tips 11

Chapter 2: Controlling Self-Talk 13
    The Power of the Negative 17
    What to Look for in Your Own Self-Talk 20
    The Value of the Negative 23
    The Many Faces of Self-Talk 26
    Your Self-Talk Affects Others 29
    What Now? 30
    Toolbox Tips 33

Chapter 3: Eliminating Distractions 35
    The Danger of Distractions 39

Identify and Control Distractions........................41
Intense Distraction..43
The Trunk Card 44
What Now?...48
Toolbox Tips..48

Chapter 4: Imagining Success........................49
Visualization at Work.....................................53
The Magic Wand..55
The Success Equation 62
Programming the Outcome 65
What Now?...67
Toolbox Tips..68

Chapter 5: Working Backward 69
Rethinking Your Business..................................74
The 180 Degree Strategy 77
Five Years Out...82
What Now?...83
Toolbox Tips..84

Chapter 6: You, Inc. 85
Don't Go It Alone...90
SWOT Analysis (Revisited) 91
Strategy #1: I Sell Mistakes.............................95
Strategy #2: The 20XX Silos.............................100
Strategy #3: The Jones Group 102
What Now?..107
Toolbox Tips..109

Chapter 7: Your Competitive Edge 111

What Is the Competitive Edge? 111

The Many Faces of Competition 113

Obstacles to Your Competitive Edge 116

The 8 Keys to a Competitive Edge 125

What Now? 127

Toolbox Tips 128

**Chapter 8: Preparing to Meet
the Competition Versus Winging It** 129

Winging It 130

Preparing to Meet the Competition 131

Knowing the Competition 132

Mistakes 134

Coaching Culture: Preparation
for a Competitive Edge 137

It Never Stops 142

What Now? 143

Toolbox Tips 144

Chapter 9: Why Stuck Is Not the Worst Place to Be 145

It's About a Lot More Than "Right Now" 147

What Now? 149

Toolbox Tips 149

**Chapter 10: Communication Strategies
for Peak Performance** 151

Common Personal Obstacles 153

The Foundations of Communication 154

Major Key #1: Effective Listening 159

Major Key #2: Effective Preparation 163

The Power of Words 175
What Now?... 176
Toolbox Tips.. 177

Appendix I: Worksheets.. 179
Worksheet I: My Toolbox... 181
Worksheet 2:   My Professional Silo 183
Worksheet 3:   My 8 Keys to a Competitive Edge 184
Worksheet 4:   My Wish List 186
Worksheet 5:   My Success.. 187
Worksheet 6:   My Self-Talk Survey 188
Worksheet 7:   My Peak Performance Zone Survey..... 190
Worksheet 8:   My Distractions Inventory.................... 192
Worksheet 9:   My Magic Wand of 20XX...................... 194
Worksheet 10:   My Success Equation............................. 197
Worksheet 11:   My ODR (Obstacles, Distractions,
                  and Resistance) 198
Worksheet 12:   My Trunk Card..201
Worksheet 13:   My Mental Success DVD.......................202
Worksheet 14:   My Skepticism Schedule 203
Worksheet 15:   My SWOT Analysis.................................204
Worksheet 16:   My @#$% List 207
Worksheet 17:   You, Inc. Resources 209
Worksheet 18:   Mistakes..212
Worksheet 19:   My Ideal Business Card 214
Worksheet 20:   My Coaching Culture 215
Worksheet 21:   My Integrated Working
                  Backward Strategy................................... 217
Worksheet 22:   My Sense of "Stuckness"........................ 219
Worksheet 23:   My Nonverbal Communication
                  Habits 222

Appendix II: Quick Table of Issues................................225

Appendix III: Additional Stories.............................229
    Create Your Own Zone:
        Hedge Fund Analyst/Trader.........................231
    In the Pool: John Repetti..............................232
    A Record Mindset: Craig Pinto......................233
    Play It Again: Jourdan Urbach......................235
    Back on Target: Charlie Blankstein...............236
    The Roar of the Crowd: Ken Davidoff...........237
    Feeling Is Not Fact: Alice Spitz, Esq.
        and Sal DeSantis, Esq......................238
    All the World's a Stage: J. Robert Spenser.......239
    Finding Your Motivation: Rohan Murphy.......240
    Every Game Is a Mind Game: Anthony Becht....242
    Building Up the Jones Group:
        The Secret Core of You, Inc. 243

**Appendix IV: Testimonials for Dr. Dan Schaefer
and the *CLICK!* System** 247

About the Author..253

Forthcoming: There's $$$$ in Mistakes 255

FOREWORD

For a variety of reasons, the 2007 season was probably my least favorite as a professional football player. But the very next season—2008—was by far the most enjoyable of my career. What changed? In the pages of this book you will find some of the things that made the difference for me. They can have the same effect on your life.

In 2007 I had a lot of time to think; that's pretty much what you get to do when you're spending time on the bench. It would have been very easy to hear myself echoing the comments of a lot of sports writers and saying my career was finished or I'd lost my touch. But that's not what I chose to do.

Instead, I reached out to Dr. Dan Schaefer. I first worked with Dr. Dan in 2005 after a shoulder injury. At that point, we used hypnosis and some other techniques to control my self-talk, restore my confidence, and help me get back in the game. But 2007 was when I really took ownership.

Once you dive into the world of professional athletics, it's no longer just about the game in between the white lines. There are many things outside those lines that can impact your play if you don't address them. In order to stay in the game—and be successful in it—you have to keep it simple. This is the biggest challenge professional athletes face. With all the variables—media attention, family responsibilities, pressure from friends, and business opportunities—it's so easy for everything to crumble. The truth is that it's not really complicated; we just tend to make it complicated. The key to athletics is to let it be straightforward—to focus on the game and let the other stuff fall away.

So much negativity surrounds an individual athlete's performance. The only way to combat it is to build a solid concept of whom and what you want to be as a professional athlete. Then every time you hear or read something negative, you have to revisit your own concept and see if the remark is true. If it is, it's a chance for you to realign yourself. If not, then it's pretty easy to dismiss.

This core concept of who you are—Dr. Dan calls it "You, Inc."—is important to the longevity and success of your career as an athlete, but the concept goes beyond the football field. It goes into family life, financial life, and business life. In all these areas success comes back to that core concept. If you don't remain true to it, you can get involved in things you have no business being in.

The techniques Dan and I have worked on over the past six years have truly helped me keep my craft at the center. Without them, I wouldn't have been able to provide for my wife and three boys. There's no manual that tells you how to be a professional athlete or how to convert your success on the field to success off the field. This book helps to fill that gap.

—Chad Pennington
NFL Quarterback
Two-Time Comeback Player of the Year
Founder, 1st and 10 Foundation
April 2011

PREFACE

Dr. Dan Schaefer's book *How Do We Tell the Children?*, now in its fourth edition, is a superb guide on helping children to cope with loss. I've recommended it to many of my clients, and they have all found it extremely helpful.

In *CLICK! The Competitive Edge*, Dr. Dan turns his mastery of the simple and the obvious, which most people, to their detriment, are distracted from seeing. He then provides tools they can utilize in business, sports, and entertainment. As a psychiatrist, I would add to that list their potential usefulness in improving self-esteem and the quality of personal relationships.

The keys he provides make eminent good sense when practiced—but first it takes practice to achieve those keys. Here are just a few examples of what he teaches: controlling negative self-talk, recognizing and eliminating distractions, and trusting your preparation. He asks you to think about what's not happening right now in your life that you want to have happen. He then instructs you on finding what there is about *you*, not others in the organization or in your life, that's getting in the way.

Think that's simple? It's not. Dr. Dan teaches you how, as

he has professional and amateur athletes and executives of all stripes. Read and utilize his wisdom and experience and stay with his program; there is much to be gained. Don't miss the worksheets in the appendix; they provide straightforward and useful tools for achieving your goals.

—David Peretz, MD
Department of Psychiatry, Columbia University College of Physicians and Surgeons; faculty, Columbia University Psychoanalytic Center for Training and Research; novelist and screenwriter

ACKNOWLEDGMENTS

Andi, Daniel, Pam, Mark, David and Shawn along with Stuart and Rachel, who exemplify caring, vision, focus, drive, and determination.

To my **Confidential Sounding Board** clients:

Special thanks for the confidence you place in me. Your willingness to engage in a process that defies conventional wisdom, focuses on winning, and involves influencing with integrity has been invaluable. The belief that it is a great idea to have someone "under the radar" at your back has enhanced your ability to gain a competitive edge in business, sports, and life.

From a board room in Australia to a hotel lobby in Geneva to a restaurant in Prague to a private club in Beijing—from Kuala Lumpur to midtown Manhattan and the slopes of Vail, you have all taught me the challenges of leadership.

Whether on the ice, snow, fairway, gridiron, in the middle of Death Valley, or in an MMA fighting cage, you've taught me how little difference there is between business and sports and how your minds have made you the champions you are.

I am certain that you will find parts of *CLICK! very* familiar. Thanks again…

The *Click!* System

Special thanks to Kyle Fager, who helped make sense out of years of stories, allowing *Click!* to become a cohesive manuscript and bringing it to the twenty-yard line.

To Steven Skyles-Mulligan, who took over in the red zone and brought it in for a touchdown. Steven has the patience of a saint and the unique ability to listen to me and translate my ideas into words that sound like me.

My thanks go as well to Larry Leichman, Jessica Gorham, and Martin McHugh at Arbor Books.

The following people had a significant impact on the development and promotion of the *Click! System*, so...sincere thanks to Will Rico, Richard Gertler, David Abeshouse, Richard Cohan, Janet Costello, Marilyn Davidoff, Lloyd Friedland, Marvin Soskil, Jody Lynn Reicher, Rory Sheehan, Alec Urbach, Allan Lipscher, Steve Goldstein, and Barrie Sue Zicherman.

And thanks to all who contributed their stories and whom you will meet as you move through the book.

INTRODUCTION

The Toolbox

Imagine…for a moment…that there is a toolbox on a table before you. It has your name on it. Maybe you are consciously aware of it or, like many, just don't give it much thought. One way or the other you've had it for a very long time. In reality, whether people realize it, everyone has a tool box. Picture it as a conventional, durable toolbox not unlike the one printed on the back cover of this book.

When you open the toolbox, you find it's full of all sorts of tools, some very familiar. You know they are there, and you know when and where to use them and right where to find them when you need them. Even if you don't visit your toolbox very often, somewhere in the back of your mind you are aware you need to use the right tool to do each job. If you don't, you run the risk of doing the job badly, of taking more time than you need to, of hurting yourself, or even of making the situation worse. Not using the right tools at the right time can result in very costly personal and business mistakes.

This book is like a guide to using your toolbox to achieve specific ends. Working with it, you will gain better mastery of tools you already use in your business and in your private life. More important, it will help you understand what tools you need to acquire to achieve the outcome you want. Among them will be some you use almost every day. The book will help you use them with greater skill and finesse to get better results.

Other tools will be oddly familiar, and you'll find you have been using them instinctively without really knowing it. The book will help you get a better grasp on them so you can use them with greater purpose.

Finally, you may encounter some tools that are completely new to you, taken from personal or business situations that appear far different from your own but which, when brought on to your playing field, give you an unexpected edge and become essential to what you want to accomplish. Then you will, as professional athletes must, trust that what you've worked and trained for will provide you what you need when you need it.

Some tools may be applied to your Professional or Business Silo (for more on silos, see Chapter 6). They are called "negotiating," "analytical thinking," "litigation," "accounting," "legal analysis," "sales strategy," "management skills," and "psychological communication" to name just a few.

You are probably very familiar with the tools you use in your Personal Silo. They help you do things like build and maintain personal and business relationships, parent your children, and interact with your siblings; they help you build rapport, support friends, and set your long-range plans.

If you are thinking strategically, you may already have begun weaving a personal safety net or developing a Consulting Company Silo that brings together groups of experts to solve specific challenges. There has never been a time when this was more important than it is today. But we'll talk more about these kinds of solutions later.

For now, let's come back to the toolbox. We have already recognized the tools you are aware of. Certainly, we are also aware that there are always new tools being made available to address new challenges. It would be foolish, wouldn't you agree, not to drop these tools into your toolbox even if you didn't need them right now? Some may be readily available anytime, anywhere, and some may be needed only once.

So we know there are tools we possess and know about, and we know there are tools we know about and should probably possess. But what if there were a third category? What if there were another set of tools at our disposal?

Imagine...for a moment...that there is indeed another set of tools already in your toolbox but you can't see them. They are invisible.

These are the tools that work so well for you—and that you have used so well, so often, and with such consistently great outcomes—that you don't even realize they are there. You may have heard the expression "unconscious competence." This is what I am talking about. There are tools in your toolbox—indeed, there are a multitude of them—that you use without thinking. It is *these* tools you may want to uncover and harness if you wish to improve your performance at work, in sports, in academics, and in daily life.

The easiest place to look for examples of this unconscious dynamic is in sports, where we often see a reflex reaction to a situation, seemingly without thought. Basically, if you are an athlete, you have done certain things so well for so long that you just don't have to think about them anymore. This performance comes from your unconscious mind developed with extensive training.

Considering that you may not be an athlete or even a sports fan (and before we get too far and you begin to read analogies to sports performance), allow me to make the case as to why you may want to look to sports as a research model for performance in general. How can that be? Well, let's look at an example.

You wouldn't think that DNA research has anything in common with sports, would you? Dr. Cindy Fung was explaining research she was conducting on DNA at Harvard. I asked her what she used as a test subject, thinking it might be humans or animals, mice for example. She explained she uses yeast. Whereas it might take her months to get results from mice, she can get results from yeast in days. I immediately thought this was like sports. The convergence of time, pressure, incredible training, mind game strategies, the desire to win, and everything else involved forces the issue of getting results quickly. In fact, athletes who work with me learn to get results in a series of plays, much as Cindy gets her yeast to go through generations of evolution in days.

Now it doesn't seem so hard to extrapolate, does it?

In my experience, identifying these special, "invisible" tools has proven to be important on several different levels. In the words of many, "Initially I was skeptical, but in retrospect it was really worth the effort."

Consider this concept in a typical working environment. Whether you are a high performer, a business leader, or a new employee, knowing what you unconsciously do well can have tremendous benefits.

Say, for example, that I come to work for you, and my mindset is such that I want to learn everything about your business and create the kind of results that will justify the confidence you had in hiring me. The first thing I am going to want to know is how you get the results you do. I am less interested in the fact that you closed a big deal or won a big case than I am in how you did it, what you thought about, and how you decided to do what you did or say what you said. These things are often the keys—the tools—to why deals happen and why you are so good at what you do.

But herein lies the problem: if you do it well but are not aware of *how*, then you can't teach me what you don't know you know. Does that make sense? If you have done something so many times that the whys and hows have become unconscious, you can't help me learn the whys and hows. And if you don't know what you do well, you can't ramp it up or tone it down as necessary.

To highlight this point, I frequently use a Porsche analogy: Your Porsche may do 150, but you can't drive it flat out all the time. You have to know what it can do, when to open it up, and when to let off the gas.

What if you had a set of skills that placed you at the top of your field, producing a wonderful series of successes? If you knew how to control them, these skills would most likely be valuable in other areas of your life as well. You could use these skills in a totally different silo, but until you become aware of the skills, they remain invisible tools.

How often do you identify a real skill in someone you work with, comment on it, and then get a blank stare in return? You might even get a "Really? Do you really think so?"

I spoke recently with Alice Spitz, a partner at Molod, Spitz, and DeSantis, a New York personal injury/litigation law firm. Alice's expertise is litigation, but she told me in a casual conversation that she didn't consider herself strategic. I said, "Alice, you're very strategic. You're a litigator. I mean, what do you call what you do while you're planning and trying your cases?"

She actually paused and began to laugh.

You'd be amazed at the results people get when they bring tools from one area of their lives into another. But the task of noticing and acknowledging what you do well, the task of discovering these tools, is not without its challenges, as you might imagine. In order to uncover your hidden tools and improve your performance, you are going to have to:

1. **Compliment yourself.** As difficult as this may sound, self-congratulations are essential to the process. To succeed—in performance and in life—you must be able to compliment yourself. Not out loud, mind you, but certainly to yourself. Someone once said that God made your arms so long so you could pat yourself on the back from time to time, but far too many people have forgotten how to do this.

2. **Listen to yourself.** Plan to listen carefully to what you hear yourself saying to yourself as you compliment yourself. This will take some work, but it will be worth the effort. You'll hear a lot more about this as we move forward.

3. **Avoid getting derailed**. Imagine emerging from every challenge successfully, whether it's related to business, your performance on the field, or your presence on stage. To do this you need to develop winning strategies. But you must be able to hold these strategies even under pressure and avoid counterproductive tendencies that can derail the whole operation.

So with all that in mind, let's begin.

So why *Click!*? *Click!* is a system to quickly identify and remove anything that might impede your maximum performance.

As we move through *CLICK! The Competitive Edge,* you'll surely discover tools very familiar to you and that you have used extensively and with great success. You'll also be introduced to tools used by others—tools that some will willingly share, and others that are used constantly but are never discussed because of the edge they provide.

There is an interesting thing about the competitive edge. Once people—including my clients—realize what they have, how it works for them, and how far ahead it puts them whether in business, sports, entertainment, or life, they all seem reluctant to let others in on their secrets. This book will tell you *what* they do, just not *who* they are. This book will help you truly learn the secrets of successful people and uncover a few of your own.

Throughout *Click!* we will be looking at 8 Keys to a Competitive Edge. They are:

Mind Game Strategies
1. Control Negative Self-Talk
2. Peak Performance Zone
3. Preparation For Competition
4. Rapid Recovery

Business Performance Strategies
5. Power Communication
6. Strategic Networking
7. Influencing with Integrity
8. Long- and Short-Range Strategic Planning

At times we'll talk about these strategies individually. More often, however, they will flow in and out of stories and other strategies. You'll hear them described in the words of people who have embraced the need and strategy for change. At the end of the day, the edge is found when you recognize ways you can integrate these dynamics for your benefit into your life.

Now, before we begin, spread your arms out to your side as far as you can stretch...

Some think the six-foot space between the tips of your fingers represents the competitive edge.

Now put your thumb and index finger together and separate them just a bit...

In truth, this little space is all you need for the edge. This is where the edge lies.

Ready to begin? Okay...let's go!

Owner's Manual

Since this book can be used a variety of ways, here are a few suggestions:

1. Don't read the book. Instead, with a highlighter, review the table of contents and the appendix, highlighting topics you believe relate to a situation you are involved in right now.
2. Look through the worksheets in Appendix I and see what exercises excite you (chances are they will relate to something that has been bugging you). Then look up the worksheet in the appendix, follow the instructions, and get moving.
3. Flip through the Toolbox Tips section at

the ends of each chapter. Find the ideas that really resonate with you, note the chapters they are in, and read those chapters.

4. Read the stories in Appendix III. Decide whose stories moved you the most. Then determine what circumstances they faced—and what tools they used. Reflect on why the story appealed to you and then find material in the book that will help you dig deeper.

5. Go ahead and read the book the traditional way, front to back, but do it quickly. Keep a notebook by your side and mark down ideas that strike you. Then go back and spend more time with those ideas.

Also, as you read through the book, you'll find a couple of unusual things:

- Throughout the text I use ellipses (…) in seemingly odd places. My purpose in this is to get you to slow down and really think about the ideas here. Consider reading some of these passages multiple times—even aloud.

- You will also note some call-out boxes that start with *CLICK!* These denote something that will help you get a better grasp of the concepts I'm discussing in that section.

- Every chapter begins with a famous quote from Sun Tzu's *Art of War*. Like this book, the quote deals with the strategic art of knowledge. Look at the words that stand out in each quote, and let them play over in the back of your mind as you read that chapter.

CHAPTER 1

The Wish List

*"Know the other, **know yourself**:*
One Hundred challenges without danger;
Know not the other and yet know yourself:
One triumph for one defeat;
Know not the other and know not yourself:
Every challenge is certain peril.
Know Nature and know the Situation:
Triumph completely"
—Sun Tzu

This book is about many things, but most of all it's about you. Specifically, it's about how you can use your mind to achieve the results you want—and how you can inadvertently use your mind to get in your own way. I call the approach **Mind Game Strategies**.

As you work with me on these pages, you're going to read a lot about turning around your strategies, working backward, and imagining yourself in the future of 20XX (five years from now). But before we can even think about doing any of that, we've got to get an idea of where you stand *today*. What is it that compelled you to pick up this book in the first place? What is it you feel you need to improve within your life?

1

Imagine…for a moment…what it would take for you to come to truly know yourself. Right now. In the present day.

I gave this exercise individually to my clients—a group that ranges from athletes to entrepreneurs to business people at all levels of employment. Being my clients, these people were already working on their Mind Game Strategies, so I probably should not have been surprised to see a pattern emerging in their answers.

All of my clients come to me hoping to **improve**. Many came hoping to find an edge on the competition. And all of them were able to identify a range of things getting in the way of their achieving these important goals.

Take the time to answer two simple questions for yourself:

1. **What's not happening right now in your life that you want to have happen?**

    You can list anything here. It may be an improvement in your organizational skills. You may want to change the way you think about your daily tasks. Maybe you would like to improve your golf game or tennis match. *Anything.*

2. **What do you notice that is getting in the way?**

    Be honest with yourself here. Don't give me a list of people or occurrences that have prevented you from advancing in your career. Don't cover your lack of free time or the amount of work you are expected to do on a daily basis. What is it about *you* that is getting in the way of your achieving the things you want most in life? What would it take for you to reach your goals?

Obviously, although the questions are simple, the answers are not easy. But as you begin to do what this book will teach you and work on your Mind Game Strategies, you will start to strip away the actual business or athletic challenge facing you and address only the dynamics of your mental performance. What you will see when this happens is that there tends to be a direct correlation between the physical or logistical challenges facing people in business, sports, or the arts and the mental challenges they face every day (but maybe don't notice).

Okay... Say you buy in to this concept. You can now see where you want to go and how you are preventing yourself from getting there. What do you do? Where do you begin? How do you get results?

CLICK! This may be the single most important exercise in the entire book. It's probably also the most difficult. Do not cheat yourself by skipping over it.

The Wish List

Below are the thirteen items that came up most frequently when I put these questions to my clients. The point that struck me immediately upon putting this list together was that all of these elements my clients felt they were struggling with right now—present day—were internal in nature.

Take the time to review the **Wish List** below. I've included a few empty spaces below the thirteen points listed. This is because everyone is different, and you may feel there are other points about your mind game that need to be improved. **Write them down**. Then use the blanks to the left of each point to number these elements in order of importance to you.

Wish List

_12_ Increase Concentration
_1_ Identify and Control Self-Talk
_8_ Identify and Control Distraction
_4_ Control Anger and Stress
_7_ Increase Energy
_10_ Increase Motivation
_13_ Control Aggression
_3_ Control Discomfort
_11_ Improve Performance (on the field, in the office, in negotiations, in sales/marketing/management, etc.)
_2_ Improve Self-Esteem
_5_ Improve Self-Confidence
_9_ Identify and Resolve Subconscious Blocks
_6_ Catch Distractions Earlier

___ _____
___ _____
___ _____
___ _____
___ _____

Now you might be asking yourself What is this? Why is this important? You might feel you know what's getting in your way and writing them down is just a waste of your time.

Let me tell you, this list will come in handy as you flip

through the pages of this book. Knowing what you want, asking for it, and thinking about it are really the first steps in getting it.

CLICK! Worksheet 4: My Wish List
can help you organize your thoughts. Since
this is a "present tense" exercise, you may
want to make several copies and
go through it on a regular basis.

The Key to the Wish List

The points derived above by my clients will guide the content of this book. The process involves strategies for staying in the present. For the athlete, it's dealing with just the next shot, play or game. So let's take a look at the top 4 items most frequently selected by top performers and spend the time to explain in brief what each of them means—starting with the top and working our way down.

Increase Concentration

Almost everyone can benefit from improving this element of the Mind Game. And how do you increase concentration? The beginning of the strategy is simple: *identifying what distracts you*. But the next step can be a little more difficult: *figuring out how to eliminate those distractions*.

Distraction can get in the way of personal improvement and can prevent you from reaching the outcomes you desire. With this book, you will learn a number of strategies that will help you shut out all those distractions and *Click!* your way back to the path to those desired outcomes.

Identify and Control Self-Talk

Most of the time when I mention this term, I'm met with a blank stare. What *is* self-talk? Good question.

For some, self-talk is the constant chatter within their minds. For others, it's a little more situation-specific. Self-talk is the internal dialogue or mental audio you encounter within your mind every day. It's the way in which you *talk to yourself.*

Many people don't take the time to listen to how they talk to themselves within their minds. And if you don't take the time to listen, you'll never know whether your own self-talk is working for you or creating havoc for your performance. If you hope to achieve any kind of self-improvement, you cannot let negative self-talk get in your way.

I devote Chapter 2 to self-talk. If this topic interests you, I suggest you flip to it immediately. But the objective right now is the word "notice." Set this book down…right now…and take the time to *notice* how you talk to yourself. Keep that in mind for later.

Identify and Control Distraction

Distraction can get in the way of the outcomes you want most. But how important are these distractions?

Try this… Stand up. Support yourself by placing your left hand on the back of a chair. Now pick up your right foot and begin to rotate the tip of your foot clockwise in the air. While your right foot is going round and round—set this book down if you need to—draw a big number "6" in the air with your right hand. Move your finger across the air just as you would if you were writing the number "6" on a sheet of paper.

What happened to your foot? It reversed direction, didn't it? Okay, okay. That happens to almost everyone. The distraction of drawing that "6" is just too much to continue to focus on the actions of your foot.

The question from this exercise is not why this phenomenon happens… The question that impacts performance is, can you afford even a second of distraction? The answer most professional athletes give is no. What is distraction costing *you*?

With this book, you will learn a number of strategies that will help you identify and control distraction.

Control Anger and Stress

Of all distractions, these two tend to be the most significant. They get in the way of so many things in life, affecting performance and altering outcomes.

I have a client who is an ultramarathon runner. She is focused and talented enough to run 135 miles through the unforgiving heat of Death Valley. Personally, I can't even imagine completing one of her *training* runs: fifty miles on Saturday mornings on a regular basis. Anyway, why do I bring her up here? Well, she once told me, "I can't run well if I'm angry. It drains me."

Anger has so much power that it can bring down even one of the toughest kinds of athletes the world has ever known. So my client identified her distraction as anger. The next step was to learn a series of strategies that could help her deal with that anger at a more appropriate time—and you'll learn all about those in this book.

As for stress, there are many well-catalogued stress-management tactics, but try this one: Focus intently on a small spot on the wall directly in front of you... Got it? Okay.

Now...take a deep breath. Close your eyes and slowly count to three.

Now...open your eyes—and this is critically important—focus on the exact same spot on the wall you picked earlier.

Feel that? That's stress leaving your body. This might seem like an overly simplistic tactic, but if you are like ninety-eight percent of my clients, this actually works. When you open your eyes, you will feel the stress run out of your neck and across your shoulders.

Complete this strategy frequently, and eventually you'll find you begin doing it without even realizing it. Like many of the strategies you will learn in this book, it will begin to become subconscious, automatic. I've had clients describe situations in which they used this strategy more than once. In fact, one client measures his meetings by the number of times he had to use this blink strategy: "That was a three-blink meeting!" he would say.

***CLICK! Make the blink strategy your own—
and use it as often as you need to.***

Conrad

Ungly freaks

(3) old

What Now?

Because the mind is constantly in flux, the Wish List is not static. For most people, every day is different; each day comes with new challenges, new distractions, and new desired outcomes. The goal here is to draw from the list I have presented above and add to it any other points you would like to improve upon. Once you have done that, you can begin to select the **three most important categories** on a day-to-day basis.

For athletes, the items of importance change as they approach different opposing teams. Each week brings a new team to the table. Each new team brings a new challenge. Each challenge must be met with a new desired outcome. For business people, the change in challenges and outcomes is even more concentrated. It can happen for each meeting, each upcoming project, each sales goal, etc.

Remember, the Wish List functions in the *present day*. Which three items on the list are most important to you today? Tomorrow, ask yourself the same question. Staying in the present is critical. Do this, and you will have a system at your disposal that will help you identify and begin to eliminate anything that gets in the way of you performing at your best.

Now that we have identified your key areas of concern, let's shift gears for a minute.

Imagine...for a moment...that the changes you would like to make have already happened. What would your life look like or feel like?

Imagine...for a moment...that you could program yourself to achieve this kind of success.

Well, you can.

In the coming chapters you will be introduced to a number of elements that contribute to the Mind Game Strategies.

But for now I want you to put this book down. When you reach the bottom of this paragraph, actually **stop reading**. Spend some time imagining. Imagine you were able to focus on having a competitive edge. Imagine you were able to get exactly what you want from this book as well as from life.

> *What would your life look like?*
> *What would your life feel like?*
> *What would your life sound like?*

CLICK! Worksheet 5: My Success
presents this exercise in detail.

The pages to come will help you identify ways to **achieve the outcomes** you have discovered by answering these questions. Many of the topics will apply to you. Many will help you **improve your outcomes**, and some will not. If you are unsure of how to proceed, it is important that you take the time once again to complete the Wish List activity. It will help you identify where you stand today and what you need to do to **reach your ideal future**.

But in the meantime flip through the pages and discover the chapters that apply most to your life. Many strategies are contained in this book—there are dozens of tools you might want to put in your toolbox. Take the time to see which ones are right for you. Then you can begin *using* them.

Toolbox Tips

- Identify what you want to happen in your life *right now* that isn't happening.
- Notice how you are getting in your own way.
- Recreate your Wish List on a regular basis to keep it fresh.
- Observe the things that distract you.
- Become aware of how you talk to yourself—and when you do it.
- Practice controlling anger and stress.
- Visualize your success using each of the five senses.

CHAPTER 2

Controlling Self-Talk

*"Know the other, **know yourself**:*
One Hundred challenges without danger;
Know not the other and yet know yourself:
One triumph for one defeat;
Know not the other and know not yourself:
Every challenge is certain peril.
Know Nature and know the Situation:
Triumph completely"
—Sun Tzu

February 3, 2008: Super Bowl XLII
New York Giants 17, New England Patriots 14

Why do I kick off the chapter with this particular Super Bowl score? It's because very few people outside New York picked the Giants to win. The Patriots, only the NFL's second undefeated regular-season team, entered the contest looking unstoppable. The Giants, meanwhile, were considered huge underdogs—lucky to be playing in the game at all. It would be a rout, most people said. The Giants didn't stand a chance, they said.

I didn't agree. And there was a good reason for this. Both

individuals and teams must, at all costs, avoid telling themselves what they **don't** want to have happen. This is because, when you tell yourself you don't want to do something, your subconscious mind usually fails to hear the "don't" part, and what you were hoping to avoid in the first place winds up happening.

The New England Patriots, staring at the most significant undefeated season in NFL history, seemed to be telling themselves all week (evidenced by their media sessions, their interviews, and their practices) that they didn't want to lose this game. The Giants, meanwhile, took a more positive approach. They were predicting victory—some of them even going so far as to guarantee it.

So what was the outcome? The Patriots **found a way to lose**. They were fueled so fully by what I call negative self-talk that they were simply outmatched by their opponents.

But what is negative self-talk?

I have done a lot of sessions and a lot of seminars with a lot of people. And what I have found is the way we talk to ourselves, or "self-talk," has the biggest effect on our mind game, which in turn has the biggest effect on our daily performance. If your inner monologue is on a negative track (and as we'll see later, this negative monologue can be either conscious or subconscious), you are almost certain to fall short of your goals.

But before we get into all that, we need to figure out what your self-talk sounds like. How do you do that? Well, in a second I'm going to ask you to put this book down and ask you to:

Imagine…for a moment…that you are eavesdropping on your own internal conversations. When you do this, you must listen to and note the content. Take careful note of the words you use when you talk to yourself.

Listen for a minute… What do you hear? Pay no attention to the environmental noise that surrounds you every day. Listen only to your own mind. What do you hear yourself saying to yourself?

Okay. Now put this book down and **listen**.

So did you like what you heard? If the answer is yes, that's fantastic. At the moment you don't have to worry about negative self-talk. But answer these next questions truthfully:

What do you think your self-talk sounds like when you are nervous?

- Anxious?
- Stressed?
- Behind on a deadline?
- Up against tough competition?

It probably sounds a little different, doesn't it? If you didn't like your self-talk, your first question might be, "Why does it even matter?" or "Why even take the time to look at this?"

There are a plenty of reasons, the first and most obvious being that it just doesn't make sense to listen to negative self-talk all the time.

Imagine…for a moment…that you're in Manhattan, having a fantastic dinner at a five-star restaurant. You drove there, so you've parked with a valet. When you exit the restaurant, you hand the attendant your ticket and wait for him to retrieve your car. A few minutes of standing in the cold later, you see your car swing around the drive and pull in at your feet. The valet leaves the engine running and (it sounds like) the stereo blasting. You thank and tip the valet, then climb inside your car.

As it turns out, you were right about the music. It is loud, and it is annoying. In fact, it seems the kind of music you hate the most is exactly the kind the valet loves the most.

Imagine...for a moment...that instead of doing anything about the awful music you just put the car in drive and travel the 150 miles to Montauk, at the eastern tip of Long Island.

Sounds ridiculous, doesn't it? Nobody does that. Nobody drives for hours while listening to music he or she hates. What would *you* do?

Let me tell you what you wouldn't do: you wouldn't find yourself in Southampton—a little more than halfway to your destination and an hour and a half into your drive—saying, "This awful music is still playing." No, instead, you would have changed the station to something you enjoy before you even pulled away from the restaurant. And it's so simple! You can do this because you have AM and FM, XM and Sirius. You've got CDs and MP3s and iPods and all sorts of useful music tools.

So why is it whenever most people find bad soundtracks playing in their heads they don't simply change the channel? I'm not talking about music, now. I'm talking about **the way we talk to ourselves**. Whenever most people get to thinking about something negative, that internal tape of negativity just seems to play and play and play.

Let's talk about you, though. If it is at all possible your self-talk is negative enough to contaminate your performance, take you off your game, force you to lose your focus and concentration, sap your self-confidence, or set you up for failure, then you may want to consider doing something about it...quickly.

And *quickly* is the key here. Why? Great question. Here's the answer:

You can't control what you can't hear, see, or feel. Since most people don't take the time to listen to, look for, or feel what their self-talk is doing to them, they find that there are many things in life they have a hard time controlling. And the longer you let any potentially negative self-talk go unchecked, the more likely it is you will fall short of your talents, capabilities, and expectations.

So you have to buy into this in order for it to work. Most people don't have the kind of quick-fix solutions to negative self-talk that equate to changing a radio station or sliding in a favorite CD. Fortunately, this book is full of **mind game strategies that work**. But again, you have to believe in the power of self-talk and your ability to change it for the better. As you will see as we move on, these strategies might help not only the way you perform but also the way people at work or at home or on your team perform as well. Whether in business, sports, or entertainment, this strategy will have value for you and those with whom you interact.

The Power of the Negative

There is a tradition in most professional sports called "trash talking." The idea is that athletes will talk negatively to opponents in the hopes of breaking their concentration. If the opponents aren't concentrating, they will be off their game. The opponents' performance drops considerably, and the trash talkers' chances of gaining the advantage improve dramatically.

I have worked with and interviewed a lot of athletes who see it and hear it all the time, and they all say the same thing: trash talk *definitely* works!

So why should it be a surprise that it can work on you

as well? It's one thing to hear the linebacker across from you telling you that you aren't going to make that first down, but it's quite another matter if **you yourself are saying it**. Actually, you could say trash talking yourself (listening to negative self-talk) is even more damaging than hearing it from someone else. There are three reasons for this:

1. Negative self-talk is in **your own voice...** We tend to believe ourselves long before we believe others.
2. For most people, negative self-talk is **harder to control**... There just doesn't seem to be a way to block it out or shut it off.
3. For some people, negative self-talk is **relentless**... It plays for days, weeks, and even years.

The most subtle form of negative self-talk was highlighted in the anecdote I used to open this chapter. You must avoid telling yourself at all costs what you *don't* want to happen. The Patriots lost because in part they were telling themselves they didn't want to lose. If you have a major presentation coming up, you can't tell yourself not to be nervous and still expect not to get nervous. If you have a trial, you can't tell yourself not to lose the jury, or you'll lose the jury. Ask any golfer what happens when he or she thinks *I don't want this ball to go into the water.* Seven times out of ten it goes right in the water.

Still don't buy it? Let's put the shoe on the other foot.

Think about your competition. No matter what your field, they are the ones standing between you and **ultimate success**. How do you hope they are talking to themselves? What would you like to hear them say when they think about their chances against you? What kind of self-talk do you hope runs through their minds on a consistent basis?

This negative self-talk risk can be costly in business. It's bad enough if just the CEO is speaking this way to himself or herself, but if that mentality spills over to the sales or business development team—or worse yet, to the clients—the cost can be dramatic.

There is, however a greater problem. Because negative self-talk is often unrecognized—and even less likely to be discussed when it is—people have a tendency to notice unfavorable outcomes without knowing what brought them into being.

Answer truthfully the following questions:

- Are there any outcomes in your business or your life that did not live up to your hopes or expectations?
- What's not happening that needs to be happening right now?
- If you and your team have tried everything you can think of to succeed but are still not getting the results you want, is it possible that something else is getting in the way?

It's possible that you are experiencing a backlash from negative self-talk whether you hear it or not. Make no mistake, just because you do not recognize something as a threat does not mean it is not a threat. A significant one.

What to Look for in Your Own Self-Talk

Let's move now to a few exercises designed to get you thinking about the way you talk to yourself. Once we have established patterns in your self-talk, we can determine ways to break them or use them to your advantage.

As with everything, we begin by *noticing* and *listening*.

What are you listening for? Good question. When you put down this book and take the time to examine your self-talk, be sure to note these specific things:

- Listen to the words you use to talk to yourself.
- Listen to and note the content of your talk.
- Listen, no matter how horrible things might get.

This last point is important… You must not pass judgment on what you say to yourself. For now, just listen. There's a good reason for this. Let's say you hear yourself saying some pretty horrible things in your mind. If you simply say, "I shouldn't be talking to myself this way" and then stop listening, you will miss the story of your self-talk. You will miss the point entirely.

Don't judge now… Wait until later to do that.

For now, let's take the time to note a few things you are saying to yourself today. At this very moment. What I am going to ask you to do is take another few minutes to listen to your self-talk. Specifically, I am going to have you note three statements that you hear yourself making in your own mind.

Put the book down again.

Now write down three things you said to yourself:

1. _____
2. _____
3. _____

For today, you might find the statements are positive or even inconclusive—you are currently doing some independent reading, after all. But if you compare your notes today with the notes you collect over the next month, you are sure to find significant differences. More important, whenever you are **faced with a challenge** you must meet, you might stumble across some patterns that get in the way of your performance.

So remember this exercise. The next time you have a sales meeting or a trial or a surgery or a ball game, listen to your self-talk. Then note three statements you hear yourself making:

1. _____
2. _____
3. _____

When you have your statements, choose another situation and repeat the exercise. In a month you will have many such situations and many lists of self-talk statements to study.

---

*CLICK! Spend some time with Worksheet 6:
My Self-Talk Survey. While you do not
need to complete the full worksheet every
day of this month of observation, you may
want to complete it once per week.*

During this month of examination and listening, there are a few other things you should notice and look for whenever your negativity tape begins to play as well. When you hear yourself getting negative, ask yourself these questions:

- When did this internal conversation start? (Try to be as exact about the time as possible.)
- What day of the week is it?
- What started it? (If you aren't sure, that's fine.)
- What's going on around you?
- Where are you?
- Who are you with?
- What are you doing?
- How long does the self-talk last?
- How loud is it?
- What if anything causes it to stop? (Again, if you aren't sure, that's fine.)
- Did you do anything yourself to cause it to stop?
- Does it simply fade out?
- Is it in your own voice?
- Is it always in your own voice?
- If not, whose voice is it?

These are important questions to answer, as you may discover that certain situations produce very specific and consistent self-talk.

You might find yourself looking at all your answers and thinking, *Wow, I really harp on myself. All my self-talk is negative.* Don't be discouraged. You have learned a great deal about yourself that will be useful as we move forward. And besides, not all negative self-talk is harmful. In fact, some can be used to your benefit.

The Value of the Negative

Listen carefully... Not all negative (sounding) self-talk is contaminating. Your internal conversation may be self-critical, but so what? There's a chance that it's right on.

Now I'm not talking about statements such as "I'm useless" or "I'll never get this project done" here. Those are certainly damaging—and we will talk about ways to weed these kinds of statements out. I'm referring to specific statements you might hear like "I'm not prepared" or "I'm not going to do well on this." Many times these sorts of self-talk statements have a way of becoming quite accurate.

When you hear these things, you must ask yourself a few questions. *Did I prepare?* is among them. Of course, there are many questions to ask whether your business or personal or athletic "stuff" is not working quite the way you planned or if a performance or program is bleeding. And no matter how painful the answers might be, you have to ask them. The sooner they are asked, the sooner you can stop that bleeding.

Many people say, "I don't know what questions to ask." This is a fair statement, but you don't know the questions only if you aren't listening to yourself. There is a part of you that knows the right questions, and there is a part of you that doesn't want to hear the answers to those questions. There is a positive/constructive and negative/destructive side to every internal conversation, to every occurrence of self-talk. It is up to you to get beyond the discomfort and push towards resolution.

Here's a solution that some say works exceptionally well. You may want to try it. When you get conflicting answers, as we do in all kinds of situations we confront, try this:

Act as a moderator between your positive and negative sides. Don't dread, but encourage the two conflicting viewpoints you discover inside you to enter into a debate. You, the level-headed one looking for resolution, act as referee.

This might sound crazy, but it really works.

Ask questions of both your positive and your negative sides. Listen to the replies. Take notes on the replies.

When you're done, look at your notes. Do you see anything that says what you *don't* want to have happen? Underline those phrases, circle them, highlight them, whatever you need to do. These are the damaging phrases you must work to overcome.

Don't worry if this seems difficult. Facing your negative side and asking the tough questions of yourself is *always* difficult. The answers you come up with might lead to solutions you find uncomfortable. But this is the only way to improve performance—make the sacrifices.

I have a client who recently had to make sacrifices he didn't quite enjoy. These days he calls himself "Mr. Invisible," and there's an interesting story behind that.

To set the stage: I have five kids, and like any parent reading this, I would do anything to help them and to protect them. Mr. Invisible is the same way. He has a son who is clearly a great high school hockey player. Unfortunately, several months ago, his son's coach didn't seem to see things that way. This talented young man just wasn't getting the playing time his father thought he deserved.

Before Mr. Invisible became Mr. Invisible, a friend of his suggested he call me because he had heard I work with professional athletes in complete confidentiality (I call this working under the radar), to improve their performance. Desperate for solutions, he gave me a call.

"My son has been benched," he told me. "I'm furious. I've confronted the coach. I sit close to the bench. I just don't know how to get through to this guy."

Any parent will be able to relate to Mr. Invisible's next words. Though he was describing a problem *he* was having, he was worried only about his son. "Can you see my son and help him?" he asked.

I agreed to talk to his son. The kid was great. He picked up some unusual strategies to **focus, concentrate**, and **control his self-talk**. He loved them and was excited to give them a try. But as we talked, it became clear that his troubles on the ice involved more than sports performance. He was dealing with an issue of interpersonal politics.

Long story short, it seemed this young man's playing time hinged on whether he gave the coach what he wanted. Play the way the coach wanted, you play. Don't, and you don't play. Coach wins. Simple as that.

So we ended the meeting. The kid went to wait outside my office while I had one last word with his father. Mr. Invisible suggested to me that he and his wife would be taking further administrative action on the coach. I nodded and wished him luck. Of course, his son didn't know about any of this—and he certainly wouldn't have agreed to it had he known.

But as he turned to leave, the proud father asked me if I thought there was anything he could do to help his son.

I smiled and told him he would have to do the opposite of

what he had been doing. "Become quiet and invisible," I said. In Brooklyn, that kind of statement sounds like, "Shut up and disappear."

The father still laughs about this today—but mostly because the results were overwhelmingly positive in the long run, even if he had to take the discomfort and overcome his negative self-talk regarding the coach. Here's what he recently told me about the situation:

"My son, not me, transformed his relationship with his coach. I continue to follow your advice... I'm Mr. Invisible.

"The coach continues to try to motivate his players using fear and control. 'Do what I say or you'll be benched.' So I asked my son if he ever lets an opposing player get in his head the way he let the coach get in his head... He said that he never does, and that he can now bring the same mental toughness to whatever his coach says or doesn't say. Breakthrough!

"My son now sees that self-confidence is something that no one other than himself can take away."

The Many Faces of Self-Talk

I was once asked to meet with an individual who put himself out there as a highly successful lender. Basically, he seemed to be attempting to project the image of a man with a great deal of money and sway.

As we ate lunch, I started to get the feeling the story he was telling had gaping holes in it. Red flags began to fly, but I ignored them. All throughout the meal I was getting more and more uneasy about this guy, but I kept on. It shouldn't have been surprising to hear him thank me for lunch as soon as the bill arrived, but it was. "Thanks for lunch, Dan," he said—as if

I had offered to buy him lunch in the first place. Respectfully (but feeling a little burned), I paid the bill.

When we got up to leave the restaurant, I did something I had never done consciously before: I looked at his shoes. They were old, dirty, and scuffed—probably not shined in months. So I had basically just been conned into a free lunch by a man pretending to be far more successful than he actually was. And the worst part was that *I could sense it* before I even knew it was true.

Long story short, the discomfort I was feeling during the meal proved lethal to deals others conducted with this man. For those who picked up the negative sense projected by this man (and followed their intuition about it), a painful deal was avoided. For those who did not pick up on it, things became very costly in the end.

So what's the point of this story? Intuition. And the reason I bring up intuition is that it is a form of self-talk.

Is self-talk always talk? Absolutely not. Will you always hear words during this internal conversation? Not necessarily.

I have spoken to people who say they are not aware of self-talk but are very aware of the way they *feel* in a situation. A client in her sixties who wanted to ramp up her mind game for her marathons confessed, "I don't hear any self-talk. I just *feel* stuff."

Intuition is only the beginning. The way we feel our self-talk can take many forms. Take intimidation, for example. Another client of mine suggested he just doesn't play well fifty yards in on the golf course. He starts to feel very poorly about his chances of success once he gets within fifty yards of a hole.

"The worst part," he told me, "is that it happens only when I'm playing other people. When I'm alone, I'm fine from fifty yards in."

So my client and I discovered he feels this way only when he plays against other people. More specifically—and more interestingly—he feels intimidated only when he plays with people who *make more money than he does*. And this guy makes seven figures, by the way.

Once we had ironed out his strategies for overcoming his golf-related self-talk, we discussed how his intimidation might also be affecting his business negotiations. If he can't golf under the pressure of playing people who make more money than he does, how well can he negotiate with these same people?

Sometimes self-talk is all about energy...intuition...vibes.

Why is this? Because intuition is an instinctual device designed to protect us from dangerous situations. Whether our dangerous situation is making a bad business deal, going over the middle to catch a pass, or remembering our spouse's birthday, intuition plays **a major role** in our lives.

Paying attention to our own protective devices can prove difficult and valuable at the same time. Many books have been written about people who "just felt something," over-rode the feeling, and then found themselves in trouble. When addressing negative self-talk, an effort needs to be made to pay attention to these feelings.

Women are miles ahead of men in this department... Why? Because they already *pay attention*. Count me among the men who are consistently amazed at how on target women tend to be. Over and over in my office I hear, "Doc, she was right again."

How do they do it? I'm not sure. But I've learned to pay attention to the phenomenon. I'm not just talking about small, insignificant, everyday stuff either.

I'm good, but my fiancée, Barrie Sue, is better, and I've learned to listen. Not so long ago I spoke to a colleague who has an impressive background in international intelligence. He had just experienced a bad situation with a client. He told me, "My wife only has to listen to a voice on the phone and she gets it. One short conversation with this guy and she knew he was bad news. Dan, I should have listened," he said, shaking his head.

What do people pick up? Con artists, gaps in stories, stories that just don't compute. Remember the story about the guy with the worn-out shoes who conned me into buying lunch—and conned others out of a lot of money? Always honor your intuition.

In the end, not listening…not paying attention to your intuition can get you in trouble. When you do get the vibe, run, don't walk, away from the situation.

Your Self-Talk Affects Others

The most damaging part about self-talk is that the way we talk to ourselves tends to be the way we talk to others on any team or in any group we may be a part of.

In working with the Colorado Ski Team a few years ago, I noticed a few things about the damage negative self-talk can do. Late in the afternoon, after each racing practice (when everyone in the room was exhausted to begin with), the team's members would be shown videos of their performances. Over and over again the coach would point out the errors each skier had made in running the gates.

Here is the reality of the situation… If I wanted to make sure an athlete performed *poorly*, I would continually implant an image in that athlete's mind of a less-than-perfect performance. If I wanted to make each skier on my team *worse*, I would be sure to do exactly as this coach was doing. Over and over I would present them with video evidence of how terribly they tend to perform.

So my advice to this coach was to change the message. Instead, he was to begin the sessions by pointing out what each member of the team had done well. Then he could move on to the errors—which he would no longer present as errors. Instead, he was to discuss these mistakes in a positive way. He was to suggest what each skier might do *differently*. There would be no negative commands.

As the coach learned, the words "Don't do that," can be the most damaging words an athlete can hear. And in the business world, "Don't do that," can cost a fortune.

CLICK! Almost anything you say—or hear being said to you—can become a command. Be especially careful about this if you need to motivate others to perform well.

What Now?

Now that we have identified how prevalent and damaging your negative self-talk can be, we must move on to discuss ways you can overcome it. In the pages to come you will learn many solutions to developing an alternative to your negative self-talk and overcoming any performance obstacles you may be experiencing. You will learn such mind game strategies as:

- Creating a positive self-talk tape that you can *Click!* into your mind whenever negativity starts to build
- Eliminating distractions that can lead to damaging self-talk
- Imagining success
- Working backward from that successful future in 20XX (five years from now).
- Thinking of yourself as the CEO of a company: You, Inc.
- Preparing, preparing, preparing
- Communicating with yourself and with others in order to achieve success

But for now the first step is to determine how you talk to yourself. Without that knowledge, few strategies in this book will work for you. If you have trouble just listening to your thoughts, literally talk to yourself out loud. Even if you have to retreat to a private place, don't be afraid to speak aloud to yourself. These days, with cell phones and Bluetooth earpieces, you can talk to yourself *while* moving your lips and nobody will think you're crazy anyway.

If you are still not convinced of the power of negativity, I have one final story for you.

I was working with a senior executive at a global company in Geneva. This executive was responsible for the profitability of the company's operations in Ireland. I began working with him initially to determine a strategy to bring him and his entire team to the next level within the company. When our first meeting was over, the executive pulled me aside.

"I know you work with athletes," he said. "Before you go, could you help me with my golf game?"

I agreed to help. Even though he was a three handicap, I was confident my strategies could help him improve. So I told him to spend a couple of weeks listening to the way he talks to himself and then get back to me.

Long story short, the executive didn't think much of the idea at the time. In fact, he kind of scoffed at it.

Then a month went by, and I got a call from him. He told me he had signed up for a club championship and had been paired with two excellent players, both of them scratch golfers. He revealed that the closer and closer he got to the tournament, the more he heard himself thinking, *These guys are going to embarrass me.* It got so bad in fact that at one point before the first round started he said to one of the other players, "Boy, I hope you guys don't mind playing with a lousy golfer today."

Now, this client was not a lousy golfer. On that day, though, he shot a ninety-two. What he didn't want to have happen happened.

"But that's not why I'm calling," he said. "What really got me to call you is that I heard the same negative stuff on the way to negotiate a multimillion dollar contract the other day. I knew then I had to get control of this."

My client makes a great point. For most, golf is unimportant. Business success is what drives most of us. So if negative self-talk can affect my golfer client so dramatically, how can it affect the way you do business? More important, what if all this stuff affects the bottom line?

Toolbox Tips

- Pay close attention to the way you speak to yourself:
    - In general, and
    - During times when performance is critical.
- Identify times when you are likely to pose a threat to yourself simply because of the way you speak to yourself.
- Practice turning off negative self-talk.
- Act as moderator between your positive and your negative selves.
- Listen to your intuition; chances are it's trying to tell you something.
- Notice especially the self-talk that isn't verbal.
- Watch how what you say—and what you hear—has a tendency to become a command.
- Practice giving yourself positive commands out loud, especially when you're in a pressure situation.

CHAPTER 3

Eliminating Distractions

"Know the other, know yourself:
One Hundred challenges without danger;
Know not the other and yet know yourself:
One triumph for one defeat;
Know not the other and know not yourself:
Every challenge is certain peril.
*Know Nature and **know the Situation**:*
Triumph completely"
—Sun Tzu

If you've ever watched a sport, you've heard of the "zone," or something I call the **Peak Performance Zone**. It's that seemingly unconscious state in which a player can do no wrong. Every move is successful. Every shot goes in. Every hole is mastered. All seemingly without effort.

Even if you've never watched a sport, you might have still encountered the zone in your everyday life. Everything at work seems easier. One thing after another goes your way. And there's just no slowing you down. The Peak Performance Zone is an extraordinary state of being, and the best part about it is that it's one you can harness if you learn how to *Click!* it on.

The first step to figuring out how to get into the Peak Performance Zone is to figure out the answer to a few simple questions. First, how do you know when you're *in* the zone? How do you know when you're *out* of the zone? And finally... *why* does it make a difference?

Before we answer these questions, consider what other people say about their own experiences with the Peak Performance Zone:

Ultramarathoner **Jody Lynn Reicher** is a Badwater veteran and current North American 24-Hour Women's Treadmill record holder (she has also gone on to compete very effectively in mixed martial arts). She reports that when she's in the zone, everything moves effortlessly. There are no feelings in the movement. Everything seems to move at once. Time passes unnoticed. Sections of the ultraevent are over, but she doesn't remember them. She is unaware of anything outside the current feeling in the event right at that moment. Clips of her life or thoughts not related to the event can occupy her mind for minutes or hours on end without distracting her from the tasks at hand. Thoughts ebb and flow with ease. There may be pain, but she does not notice it. Time just passes.

On the other hand, when she's out of the zone, *everything* seems impossible. She notices everything outside of her. Time drags. The grass is always greener. It's hell. She's pained, she's suffering, and she knows it.

Attorney **Alan Schwartz** (law offices of Alan J. Schwartz, P.C.) describes the zone as being like no other feeling. To him it's like the beginning of a sci-fi movie, when the spaceship is running at warp speed and everything outside the zone is a blur. It's also not unlike a photograph with a very shallow depth of field in which only the limited, primary target is in focus and everything else is a soft, hazy blur.

When he's out of the zone, though, nothing seems right. Work seems endless, and no matter what he does he never makes any progress. He reports it feels like his feet are cemented to the ground.

I recently asked a **professional golfer** about how he would describe the zone. He said when he's at his peak performance, all sound seems to disappear. He often hears music rather than the normal chatter of the crowd at a match. And the round always goes quickly.

A **world cup skier** describes the feeling that occurs when the start count moves from five to one. His vision changes, and it seems as if he is looking through a short piece of PVC pipe. He recalls seeing only the first pole and is usually aware only of the sound of his skis on the snow. The race seems to be over in seconds.

I have a client who is an **NHL goaltender**. When he's playing at his best, he hardly hears the crowd. Plays move very slowly, and the puck seems the size of a dinner plate. Another client who is a **competitive rower** knows he's in the zone when he can hear nothing but the bubbles under the boat.

As for me, the best way I can describe what it's like to be in the Peak Performance Zone is that I have a surreal, focused, and confident feeling where I lose track of time and everything around me except for the task at hand.

These people—and many others—have had this sort of experience in many different situations: arguing on behalf of a client in court, working out, playing golf or tennis or bike riding. Essentially, when people get in their zone, they are extremely focused and act without having to think or second-guess what they are doing. It's almost like being on autopilot.

So…identifying your **Personal Performance Zone** experience is the first step in being able to recall and to return to that state when necessary. To identify it, we need to answer a few questions.

Recall what it's like to be in the zone. Then ask yourself the following questions about that state of being:

1. What do you hear? What sounds disappear?
2. What do you see? What happens to clarity?
3. What do you feel like inside?
4. What do you feel like outside?
5. What do you smell?
6. What happens to time? Does it slow down or speed up?
7. What happens to the speed of things? Do they slow down or speed up?
8. What did you do to turn it on? (What is your *Click!*?)

This last question might be difficult to answer, but let me give you some examples of what I mean by the *Click!* For an NFL quarterback, the *Click!* is the act of pulling on his chin strap. A trauma surgeon I know uses his right hand to snap the end of the surgical glove on his left hand. A litigator emphatically places his brief case down on the table. These small actions are a way for these top performers to signal to themselves that the action is about to begin.

Many people operate just fine without a Peak Performance Zone. But the reason we need to be in our Peak Performance Zone is because it allows us to perform at our absolute best. And performing at our absolute best is all about eliminating distractions.

CLICK! Use Worksheet 7:
My Peak Performance Zone Survey to capture
what it's like when you are in your own Zone.

The Danger of Distractions

I have a friend in Chicago with an unusual job. Jack Schultz is a security expert, and he's a safecracker. He is hired by banks and companies that manufacture safes to put their products to the test. The idea is if the safe is strong and complex enough to keep a professional safecracker out, then a thief with a limited time frame doesn't stand a chance.

My friend views his job as a kind of game, a game he calls "us against the product." For him and his partners, the mantra is "We're better than the product. We can beat this." And many times they do just that; they outperform the manufacturer's testing. But it is an important job, a stressful one, because they are the only thing standing in the way of a manufacturer getting a passing grade. If they slip up or lose their focus, a manufacturer might wind up getting a passing grade that isn't deserved. And they get only one shot. If they fall short, they fail. The product wins.

One particular challenge came up with a safe manufacturer in Chicago that had designed a product they claimed to be unbreakable. Before going to market, they hired my friend the safecracker to put it to the test. My friend and his team were given thirty minutes to crack the safe and were told that it was essentially a waste of time—that no one could break the hinges in that kind of time frame.

The team managed to break into the safe in only twenty minutes. They laid the safe on its back and worked on the hinges. Twenty minutes later, they stood it up again, and the door just fell off. The supposedly unbreakable weld had failed.

Now, my friend would say it had nothing to do with the quality of the product and everything to do with the performance of the safecrackers. When you are racing against the clock, it is essential to eliminate all distraction. When in the zone, the safecracker and his team could tune out the rest of the world and become very focused on the task at hand. Sound, sights—anything—just goes away. For this reason a third person on the team acts as a safety. When my friend and his partner are in the zone, they ignore everything. Molten metal from their torches could land on their oxygen tanks and they might not even notice.

Having to change strategies on the fly can be a distraction. Molten metal in your glove can be a distraction. Pain is a distraction. Fatigue is a distraction. Health can be a distraction. All of these things have to be tuned out. The focus must always be "What do we have to do to get to the other side?"

I have a client who is an attorney. We'll call him Sal. Sal once described to me these "vibes" he has during a trial. He'll see a turning point in a case, get a vibe, and then use that vibe as justification to go against conventional wisdom. More often than not the vibe pays off. But in order to follow it he must control the distraction that is second-guessing himself. Comes down to trusting yourself.

The way he does this is through positive self-talk. He avoids negative thoughts because they always interfere with the game plan he's devised for the case. Sal's greatest distractions come from considering whether his adversary's opinions are more logical or compelling than his own. Other distractions include the case veering off in a direction he didn't anticipate;

no matter how much preparation he does, things always seem to go differently in the courtroom. The judge usually reacts otherwise than anticipated: the plaintiff's attorney does something unexpected; the jury seems to respond in a way he did not foresee; witnesses fly off the handle.

All these things are distractions, and they all threaten to derail his cases. But when Sal is in his zone and has eliminated all distractions, he follows his game plan and attempts to make his evidence and arguments match the plaintiff's.

Sal's story is important because it speaks to the way negative self-talk can influence performance: the minute you start asking yourself *Am I doing this right?* you're sunk. You must eliminate distractions and return to the point athletes call the zone—the point when you don't even have to think about what you're doing, you just do it. The goalie doesn't need to think about putting his glove up to stop the puck, it just happens. The quarterback doesn't have to think about where to put the ball for the receiver to catch, he just puts it there.

Identify and Control Distractions

How is your own concentration? Let's take a look:

1. Sit up straight…
2. Start moving your right foot clockwise…
3. Got it going?
4. Now with the index finger of your right hand, draw a big number 6 in the air…

What happened? Your right foot started going backward, didn't it?

Don't worry; it happens to everybody. The reason it went

backward isn't important. Only the fact it happened is important. What this exercise proves is that the mind isn't built to do two different things in the same moment. The motion you attempted with your finger became a distraction to the motion you began with your foot. Unless you can find ways to block this distraction, you'll never perform the motion as you're supposed to.

CLICK! In a world where there is so much input, distractions can really prevent us from following through with our intentions.

So what are some other common distractions?

- Negative self-talk
- Stress
- Fear of interpersonal or media communication
- Anger and aggression
- Lack of energy
- Lack of motivation
- Distress about the future
- Discomfort
- Low self-esteem
- Lack of a strategic plan
- Subconscious blocks
- Lack of imagination
- Lack of persistence
- Skepticism
- Impatience

Each of these items can act either as a distraction in itself or become a distraction when you don't take steps to address and eliminate them.

Noticing starts the process…

CLICK! Use Worksheet 8:
My Distractions Inventory right now
to list your distractions.

Intense Distraction

In Chapter 1 we talked a bit about distraction, and I promised it would come up again. Truthfully, the many obstacles we face in trying to accomplish what is important to us are only distractions. So whether on the golf course or in the office, we are not likely to perform at our highest level if we are distracted by the many obstacles…real or imagined…seen or unseen… that stand in our way. For that reason we must work on three things:

First, we must improve our ability and quickness in noticing *all* of our obstacles and distractions.

Second, we must work on ways to acknowledge them—see them, hear them, and feel them.

Third, we must make an effort to move these obstacles and distractions to another, more-advantageous time.

The reason it is important for you to notice the obstacles, both large and small, that clutter your daily life is because sometimes you know something isn't working right but still cannot explain why. Sometimes you can think you've got everything in place, but something still isn't working... You just don't know what it is. Simply noticing and identifying all of the things that have the potential to stand in your way will have a tremendous effect on your ability to achieve these positive outcomes, to find your success.

The second point indicates a conscious effort to engage with the obstacle or distraction: once you have noticed the distraction, can you deal with it? Can you resolve this distraction? Can you *Click!* and make it go away or just move it to another time?

And the final point is a method to eliminating this obstacle or distraction. Or rather, moving it to a better time. Basically, this step suggests that if you are staring down at a golf course— and your mind sees a bunch of junk on the course instead of a manicured green—you could say one of two things, either "Why did this happen?" or "Look, I'm just here to play this course. Move this stuff to the side so I can hit my ball." Essentially, this step indicates that you don't have to (nor should you expect to) make all your problems go away. You just have to move them to a more convenient time.

The Trunk Card

There is a time and a place for everything...and during a moment when you are supposed to be focusing on the task at hand, distractions can only hinder your ability to complete it. At the same time we cannot simply rule out or attempt to eliminate our distractions and obstacles. There is far too much to be learned from them. So we must work to find ways to simply move distractions to a better time.

One of my athlete clients and I developed a system that helped him focus on moving his distractions to another time in a more physical way.

What we had him do is write down on a note card all the things nagging at him, whether family matters, contract issues, a critical missed play in last week's game, a pestering reporter, a misquote in the paper, etc. He wrote all these distractions on this note card and kept it in the front pocket of the suit he wore on the way to his next home game. When he got to the parking lot, he opened the trunk of his car, removed the card from his pocket, and dropped it into the trunk. Then he slammed the lid. We called it the "trunk card."

This may seem rather strange, but remember, skepticism is one of the biggest impediments to change. If it works for him, *could it work for you*?

Once he had slammed the lid to his trunk, my client would make a promise to himself that he was not going to think about the issues written on that card until eight-thirty that evening. He would not even consider his distractions until well after the game and media session were over. If an issue arose, he would snap his fingers and say, "Trunk card."

This solution worked for my client very well. And it was particularly effective with the distraction of worry. On the field he was like a man possessed. He had regained his old form simply because he had taken time to write down his biggest obstacles to success and actively decide to ignore them until the time was right.

And it can work for you too.

1. Find a quiet place, without distractions...
This is an important point because it is

critical that you have the time, space, and ability to think deeply about everything that worries you or hinders your focus.

2. **Take out a note card and pen**... Or flip to the appendix, where I have a Trunk Card for you.

3. **Write down your distractions/obstacles**... You should use clear and concise words; no need to go into great detail. If you like, you can use code words or phrases (that way, anybody who comes across your card won't know what it's about). Just make sure that the notation triggers the memory of the distraction or obstacle.

4. **Find an enclosed space to lock the card away**... My client used his trunk because it was the last symbolic container before he entered the stadium—and he didn't want his problems hanging over him when he walked into the locker room. It does not have to be a trunk—although a trunk does make a satisfying and finalizing noise when slammed.

5. **Slam the door shut**... Be sure to slam your distractions into their enclosure loudly enough that you can hear a sound. This sound is a trigger for your plan to block out the distraction until the designated time.

6. **Schedule a time to revisit the distractions/ obstacles**... Make it later in the day, some time away from work when your focus does not have to be as concentrated.

CLICK! Use Worksheet 12:
My Trunk Card to list everything that
could distract you from what you need
to do right now. Then promise yourself
that you will set those distractions aside
until a specific time and place. WARNING:
Make sure you come back to the Trunk
Card when you say you are going to. Your
subconscious mind will let you delay it as
long as you keep your bargain with yourself.
If you don't, the strategy will not work.

If we can eliminate distractions, we can work to hone our ability to focus…something that builds success and moves us closer to our positive outcomes. It is this absence of distractions that we achieve by using our *Click!*

But what do we know when we are and when we are not in our zone? What does it feel like to be on your game? What does it sound like? What does it look like?

Football players have told me that when they run into the stadium they hear the roar of the crowd. They know they are on their game when the ball is snapped, and they cannot hear the crowd anymore. I have spoken to wrestlers who tell me that once they are on the mat, they can see their coach's lips moving but cannot actually hear the words. My hockey goalie client claims that he can feel every nuance of the game. The puck is the size of a dinner plate. The skier hears only the sound of her skis on the snow. A rower hears only the sound of the bubbles under his boat. And there is absolutely no crowd around them.

Such is the power of the mind to eliminate distraction,

both physical and emotional. But in order to truly eliminate distraction, we must learn a few things about ourselves.

We all know what it looks, feels, and sounds like to fail. But can we recognize those same qualities in success? Can we use our understanding of those qualities to turn failure into success?

Yes. We'll spend a lot more time on this in Chapter 4.

What Now?

Now that you've taken the time to focus on your Peak Performance Zone and to inventory your distractions, you are in a much better place to accomplish what's important to you. In the coming chapters we'll talk about one particularly destructive distraction: anger. We'll also look at how to prepare mentally for competition so you can enter your zone at will, push distractions aside, and get back on the game plan (like my friend Sal the attorney).

Toolbox Tips

- Identify exactly how your Peak Performance Zone looks, feels, smells, and tastes so you can enter it more readily.
- Develop a physical *Click!* to signify to yourself that you need to enter your zone.
- Inventory your distractions and be on guard against them.

CHAPTER 4

Imagining Success

"Know the other, know yourself:
One Hundred challenges without danger;
Know not the other and yet know yourself:
One triumph for one defeat;
Know not the other and know not yourself:
Every challenge is certain peril.
Know Nature and know the Situation:
Triumph completely"
—Sun Tzu

Many people talk about imagining success, but how do they do that? What's their secret? How do they make it happen?

Have you seen the Ameriprise Financial commercials with Dennis Hopper? There he is, sitting on a beach in a red chair straight out of the sixties, looking very much like his character from *Easy Rider*—except for the gray hair and clean shave—and talking about dreams. The campaign is called "Dreams Don't Retire," and that seems like a reasonable statement.

We are all taught as kids to set goals but avoid daydreaming. People (or parents, teachers, guidance counselors) tell us that we should have an idea about what our future should be—about what we want to be—when we grow up. But then, once we have grown up, dreaming takes a back seat. That same process of picturing our ideal future is somehow labeled as childish or unproductive or distracting. It is shut out completely. Today I am going to ask you to reverse that trend in your own mind. Imagining success points to the idea that you should never stop dreaming…never stifle your imagination.

Imagination is simply a means to picture the future—or at least what we would like the future to look like. *A truly powerful tool.* Unfortunately, we are taught from the time we are in grade school that, apart from picking the career we will pursue for the rest of our lives, this tool should be ignored or discarded—"it's simply daydreaming." The desire to avoid daydreaming may be so embedded that it could be affecting your performance at work, on the playing field, and at home.

When seeking positive and measurable outcomes, that lesson must be *set aside*.

But before we can do that, let's first take a look at (and attempt to eliminate) the most common objections to such an exercise. I will present these objections in the form of questions I get most often in my practice.

Imagination? I'm a CEO. Isn't that kids' stuff?

Ah, skepticism. It is the enemy of any real personal progress. To answer this question directly, no… Imagination is *not* kids' stuff. And about skepticism in general, the trouble with a skeptic is that he or she tends to pass on things (way too early) that might help in the long run. In other words, skepticism comes with one enormous built-in fault: what if the solution you're skeptical about winds up working? So what's the risk in not taking the time to imagine success? This risk is…what if it works?

I've never done this before… I don't do that.

I've got two names for statements like this. The first is "killer phrases." This is simply because these sorts of phrases tend to render anything and everything you haven't tried already as not worth trying. So basically you wind up never trying anything new. Having been around the professional and sports world for a long time, I can tell you one thing: The surest way to avoid any kind of advancement or progress is to keep doing exactly what you're doing. "I've never done this before," "I don't do that," "It's not worth trying," or "We don't do it that way" aren't excuses to avoid the unknown; they are *reasons* to try something new. The other name for these killer phrases is "dream stealers." You can imagine where that title comes from.

This is weird. I'm not sure I want to do this.

"This is weird" is probably one of the more common statements made during any visualization exercise. This kind of knee-jerk reaction is simply another way to say, "I fear change." You may even notice a voice from the past—your mother or a teacher, maybe—reminding you how much you need to avoid daydreaming.

Look, if there was no desire or even need for change—positive, measurable, beneficial change—you would not be reading this chapter in the first place. Of course it feels weird—you've never done it before. I promise that if you stick it out and eventually adopt the exercise, the benefits to your life and your business will not seem so weird.

I tried it… It doesn't work.

I'm not sure if it's the society we live in or the pace most businesspeople and athletes have taken on, but if something does not work immediately, we tend to abandon it. Despite the fact that this chapter contains a section called **Magic Wand**, there is no quick and easy solution to envisioning a better future and then going out and...making it happen. The tool I present you with today is not a quick fix. It is a *process*. If we are to find positive outcomes with it, we must demonstrate a deeper resolve.

This is the stupidest thing I've done.

Okay... This is certainly an honest reaction. Even better than this one is another I frequently hear: "I might be doing this, but I'm not going to tell anybody about it." Why is it as a culture we seem so quick to label visualization and imagination as "stupid"? I have my theories, the most likely one being that when we were children, imagination was called "daydreaming," and daydreaming was considered the enemy of learning and advancement. Many times as we go through this process, you will likely hear the voice of your mother, your teacher, or a particularly ferocious nun from Catholic school barking at you to quit daydreaming and pay attention to the things that "matter." This *does* matter... Pay attention to your daydreaming.

I've never been able to visualize. I can't visualize.

This one's a cop-out. Just because you may not think yourself a creative person does not mean you can't visualize. Don't believe me. Okay...if you aren't already...sit down. Picture an apple. Is it red? Yes? Good. Does it have a stem? Yes? All right, now we're getting somewhere. Does it have leaves? No? Okay, then... Take that apple and put it on your dining room table. What color is the surface of this table? Does the apple have a shadow? Does it wobble on the table?

If you can picture a simple red apple, you have the ability to visualize. If you can picture the apple in an environment with which you are familiar (your dining room table), then you have the ability to imagine. No matter how repressed the tendency may be, *almost everyone knows how to visualize.*

Visualization at Work

Now that we have moved most of your objections out of the way, let's take a stab at a quick visualization exercise. Here is your chance—maybe the first chance you have had since grade school—to daydream in a public setting. For this exercise we are going to assume that you will walk out of here today knowing that every single thing about your life is already exactly as you have always planned.

Imagine…for a moment…that the changes you would most like to make with your life have already happened.

Can you picture it? I want you to dog-ear this page, flip to the back of this book, and find Worksheet 5: My Success. Write down three things about your initial vision of your ideal future. In this survey space I want you to write what your life looks like…sounds like…and feels like.

CLICK! Use Worksheet 5:
My Success to start engaging your senses
and the powerful tool of visualization in
helping you achieve your goals.

What does that mean? I'll tell you. To explain what your future **looks like**, you should highlight things like what kind of house you live in, how your kids have grown, how beautiful your husband/wife still is, what your office at work looks like, maybe what your retirement home looks like (and where it's located), what kind of car you drive, what kind of trips you're taking, etc. Anything you can actually *see* in your mind, write down.

Now, **sounds like** is a little different. To explain what your future sounds like, you should write down the phrases you think people are most likely to say to your ultrasuccessful future self. Consider things like, "You have such a lovely home," or "Your boys/girls have grown into nice/intelligent/capable young men/women," or "What's your secret? How do you do it?"

Feels like is a whole other animal. To explain what your future feels like, you should jot down the emotions you are most likely to encounter on a daily basis. Happiness is likely to show up on most of these surveys… You can't have success without happiness. Do you have a sense of accomplishment? Pride? Fulfillment? Likely yes. You have all of those things.

So now we have a tangible picture of the future. We know what your house, job, and family are going to look like. We know what your friends, coworkers, and admirers are going to say whenever they see you. We know the feeling you will have inside on a daily basis. It is a bright future to be certain. You might not believe this now, but it is also an attainable one.

In the following two sections I offer several solutions to help you achieve this future subconsciously. Read that again… subconsciously. What I offer is not a microwave solution… What I offer is not a twelve-step program… What I offer is not measurable by tasks completed... What I offer is measurable only by **results**.

Before we begin, I want to make one more thing perfectly clear: What you are about to read is not goal setting. It is not the five-year plan. I do not expect you to imagine your ideal future, file it away somewhere, and then work hard to achieve the goals you have laid out. This method may look like a five-year plan, but in reality it is something much more powerful.

What we will be doing with the following exercises is giving your subconscious mind instructions on how to proceed towards your imagined outcomes. It will be a road map of sorts...complete with all the known and potential potholes, roadblocks, and speed traps marked.

Why use the subconscious? The reason is because one of the things your subconscious must do at every moment of every day is act out every thought, image, or idea you put into it. The subconscious, as we learned in Chapter 2, is the *vehicle* for change.

The Magic Wand

Imagine...for a moment...that you have a magic wand...

This wand is long and narrow, made of a flexible wood—like pine. It even has that familiar pine smell. Its surface is grainy but covered with a deep black veneer. Its tip is a white band of inlaid cloth that carries a print of gold lettering. The print reads "20XX" (whatever date is five years from today).

You wave this magic wand...and you find yourself standing in 20XX...five years from today.

Now, visualize your life in 20XX. What do you imagine?

- **You and your family**...five years older.
- **You and your children**...finding more and more success all the time.
- **You**...working in a job that you love.
- **You**...having narrowed the gap between work and play.
- **You**...dealing with the clients with whom you want to deal.
- **You**...benefiting from a new height of sales efficiency.
- **You**...boasting a golf handicap eight strokes lower.
- **You**...enjoying the new boat, car, or vacation—anything you want.

Can you picture this dream? Can you see this reality of 20XX? Can you play out this reality as though it were a movie in your head?

I have a friend who is an excellent golfer. He recently confessed to me that no matter how hard he tried, no matter how many times he played it, there was one particular golf course in upstate New York he could not manage. Its hills were monstrous. Its water hazards were magnetic. Its greens were too fast. His ball would *always* seem to find an awkward lie. I learned during this conversation that my friend had recently played this course and the fact that he still had not mastered its nuances was beginning to drag on his game elsewhere. He was beginning to fear that as long as he carried the thought of that one troublesome course in the back of his mind, his handicap would continue to slip. So I devised a solution to help him visualize positive outcomes on the golf course. More important, I provided him with a way to beat that one particular course giving him problems.

First, I told him to print out several copies of an aerial view map of the course in question. Most of the time one can find this sort of map on the back of the clubhouse scorecard. I asked him to take the first copy of this map and plot out, hole by hole, where his shots were going to fall if he played at his best. If he wanted his drive to land on the fairway 250 yards on the first hole, then he was to find that spot on the map and mark it with a pencil. If his next shot needed to be a seven iron to the back of the green, then he was to mark the green shot exactly where he wanted it to land.

Obviously, I suggested that my friend go through the course, plotting each stroke in succession. I also suggested that after marking where he wanted his ball to end up, he visualize that shot actually taking place.

My friend agreed to give the exercise a try. He went through the course stroke by stroke with a pencil. When he was finished, he picked up his second copy of the map and did it again. Then he completed the exercise a third time. And a fourth. And so on.

What do you guess happened when my friend faced his troubling golf course later that day? He shot a two-under seventy. When I saw him again, he professed shock and amazement. "So many of my shots were landing right where I wanted them to," he told me. Basically, by the time my friend physically reached the first tee box, it was as if he had played the course five times already that day.

So what's the point of this story? The point is that when a person visualizes an outcome as if it has already happened, the subconscious mind tends to latch onto that visualization. It tends to see and assume the outcomes happening in that way. What most occupies your mind—intentionally or unintentionally—tends to become **reality**. And when the subconscious mind begins to operate on positive assumed realities, positive *outcomes* become all but a given. Success translates into an almost mechanical process.

CLICK! Repeatedly visualizing your success
can make it effortless and almost automatic.
Use Worksheet 9: My Magic Wand of 20XX
to get the process started.

Okay... So now what?

Now that we can envision your future, we need to make that vision a part of your present subconscious. It is a bit like allowing your imagination to *create* the future...kind of like writing and directing a movie and then turning around and watching it happen on the big screen.

That sort of thing may seem difficult. Fortunately there is a method.

- **Relax...** Find a quiet place, sit down, and (once you're done reading this section) close your eyes.
- **Watch and hear yourself...** Imagine that movie screen. Some athletes suggest that the inside of their eyelids become big-screen TVs when they close them. Now imagine you are watching yourself on that screen.
- **Be there...** Imagine that you are living this

20XX reality. Have the conversations you
expect to have. Make the presentations for
work that you believe you will be making.
Spend time with your children, now grown
up.

- **See and feel the people around you...**
Who are they? Where are they? What do
they look like? How do you know them?
Who do you work with?
- **See and feel your environment...** In
your future job, do you envision an office?
What does it look like? Feel the lacquered
smoothness of your desk. Hear the hum
of your computer. Or do you see yourself
running on a beach in Bermuda and then
conducting business from your laptop in
the afternoon? See the beach. Breathe in
the salt-water smell. Feel the waves lapping
against your toes. Or do you own a company? What does your company's building
look like?
- **Remember... Sit quietly...** Close your
eyes.
- **Hear your own voice...** Imagine how you
sound as you interact with your family. Your
coworkers. Your clients. Your employees.
- **See your outcome...** Watch yourself
achieving the desired result.
- **Hear your outcome...** Hear the reaction of
the people with whom you intend to surround yourself.
- **Feel your outcome...** Picture how it will

feel when you reach your goals.

As you get into this exercise, you may find you hear your teacher's or parent's voice. It will tell you not to waste so much time on daydreaming. Expect this. Don't let it throw you. Blocking it out is important. You may want to use your *Click!* to move beyond it.

For the more visually inclined among us, I offer a more visceral method for achieving this end. You can do one or both of two things. First, turn to Worksheet 4: My Wish List and check off all the things you need to happen in your life. You may want to make copies because your wish list, like every-thing else, will change over time. You may also want to hang up your completed wish list in your home, in your car, at the office, anywhere you feel it may help to have a visual reminder, a visual cue for your positive outcomes.

CLICK! Use Worksheet 4:
My Wish List to quickly inventory what
you want to happen in your life.

The second solution is a little more low-budget. But before I get into it, let me relate a story about how subconscious visual-ization can lead to stunning results.

I had a session with a group of hockey players, many of whom were top college players and all of whom hoped to play in the NHL someday. So I told them each to buy the jersey of the team they hoped to play for in the NHL. I told them if they wanted to, they could get their name embroidered on the back of the jersey. Now all they needed to do was hang this jersey in their closet. Just hang it. There would be no need to wear it, no need to take it out every day, no need to think it over directly every time they entered the closet.

So what happened? These hockey players began unconsciously seeing the colors of those jerseys in their closets. Subconsciously their minds began to process and implement the dream of playing for that specific NHL team. And almost all of them found that their motivation on the ice improved.

A hockey jersey is probably not your thing—and I did promise you low budget. So here's what you do: Get yourself a stack of Post-It notes. On each note write a dream…or one segment of your vision of the future. If you see all your children going to the University of Wisconsin or NYU, write that down on a Post-It. If you see yourself owning your own, highly profitable company, write that down on a Post-It. If you see you and your spouse taking a second honeymoon, write that down on a Post-It.

Once you have all of your dreams down on these sticky little pieces of paper, you should arrange them into different section…groups…avenues…silos…whatever you want to call them. Have a silo for family. Have a silo for career. Have a silo for leisure.

When you are finished, take either your Wish List or Post-It notes and stick them to the wall. This may seem a little absurd, but it actually works. Once you become familiar with what the Wish List or Post-It notes say, you won't even have to read them anymore. This is when the process becomes subconscious. Just passing this little reminder of what 20XX holds for you will allow your subconscious to pick it up and process it even if you don't realize it is happening.

The Success Equation

Part of the power of this subconscious processing is that we begin to think of our present life as a path to these imagined outcomes without even knowing it. Eventually this subconscious effort evolves into something so powerful that everything that happens in your life transpires as a positive step towards your eventual goals. Every person you meet subconsciously becomes someone who might help you advance one or more of your dream silos. The tasks you perform wind up more valuable…the relationships you form more beneficial.

This time spent on imagining positive outcomes actually translates into your best opportunity for success. For the mathematically inclined, consider this equation developed by Dr. Richard Harte:

Success = Persistence + Imagination

It is such a simple equation. The trouble is that most people who are persistent tend to shun the idea of imagination. Those who have no problem imagining their futures sometimes forget that achieving their goals takes hard work and perseverance.

So there are two parts to success: being able to *see the goal* and being able to *anticipate the obstacles* standing in the way of that goal before you confront them.

The concept of obstacles is something we have yet to discuss, but they are so critical to understand if success is to be imagined and attained.

Put this chapter aside for a moment. Turn to Worksheet 10: My Success Equation. You will find an exercise with two parts, one easy and one difficult.

For both exercises you must take your imagined outcomes of 20XX and picture them once again. Once you have that picture—or movie—in your mind, you may begin.

First, take your imagined outcome. Now try to come up with all the ways the task of reaching that outcome could get screwed up. Basically, list all the mistakes that you could make or things that could get in the way of your eventual success. I have provided more blanks for this portion of the exercise, as I imagine that more obstacles than strategies will be immediately apparent.

What Gets In the Way?

1. _____
2. _____
3. _____
4. _____
5. _____
6. _____
7. _____
8. _____
9. _____
10. _____

Now that we have that out of the way, we can move on to what will work. List ten ways to achieve your goal. These strategies must be reasonable and viable and *within your grasp today.*

What works?

1. _____
2. _____
3. _____
4. _____
5. _____

You will note in the exercise that there are more spaces for the **obstacles** than there are for the **solutions**. This is simply because the obstacles tend to be so much easier to see.

Unfortunately, because of the overwhelming clarity of these kinds of obstacles, occasionally, *larger issues overshadow the smaller ones*. We may be so wrapped up in a big headache problem that we fail to recognize all the ways it's impeding our progress.

Also, consider that obstacles are really nothing more than distractions. That doesn't mean they aren't important, but we can gain a certain amount of power over them by deciding when we're going to deal with them.

CLICK! Use Worksheet 10:
My Success Equation to jot down obstacles
you are likely to face as well as the strategies
you have at your disposal right
now to overcome them.

Programming the Outcome

In order to repeat success, we must **program ourselves** to that particular outcome.

Imagine that your memory bank is a Blockbuster Video outlet. As with any video store, your mind contains bad movies and good ones. Some are lighthearted and funny, some are inspiring, some are depressing, and some are frightening.

Say you rent three movies. When you get home, what do you do? You put one of the movies in and start watching it. Twenty minutes into the movie you realize you hate it. It's depressing, not very well made or acted, and doesn't seem to fit your mood. What do you do?

You don't watch the movie for two and a half hours saying, "Oh, this is terrible! This is terrible!"

What you do is you take the video out and put in one of the others you rented. Simple.

Now why can't we do the same thing with the videos in our head? We tend to replay negative thoughts over and over again while we shove this overwhelming evidence of positive outcomes to the side.

In order to get away from this common tendency, we must burn our own DVD of success and turn to it whenever distractions become too great or doubt begins to enter our minds.

How do we do that?

Remember the last time you met with overwhelming success at work. What was the task that brought you that success?

Write it down.

What we will be doing with this information is creating a mental DVD of sorts that will serve as a remedy for great stress or distraction—and help keep you on track to imagining success.

The goaltender client I mentioned in Chapter 3 once explained to me that he could tell exactly when he had fallen out of his peak performance zone. He would look at the scoreboard. He might begin to hear the crowd. He might actually notice his family or girlfriend in the stands. He would lose focus.

Distraction would enter his mind. He would begin to focus on all the things he was doing or had done wrong. He would remember the goals he had allowed. He would remember the jeers from the crowd. He would remember the taunts from his opponents as they skated behind the net.

So my goaltender client was way ahead of the competition in that he actually *noticed* his distractions. The only trouble was that he did not know how to eliminate them. So I sat down with this goaltender and set out to create a Best Saves DVD.

"Imagine yourself...making the best save you've ever made," I told him.

He nodded.

"Now imagine yourself...making that same save. Only this time view yourself from behind the net."

He nodded again.

"Now imagine yourself...making that same save. This time view yourself from within the net."

He nodded a third time.

"Now imagine yourself...making that same save. This time view yourself from above the net."

Once more he nodded.

We repeated this process again and again until we had many angles of this spectacular save. Save after save was made in my client's mind. He began to smile.

I told him to burn that series of saves to his mental DVD. On the way to each game, in the locker room, on the plane, in the hotel, wherever, no matter how distracted or nervous he was, he could always eliminate the distraction of self-doubt by watching this Best Saves DVD in his mind.

Now take the task you wrote above and imagine yourself completing it from your own perspective. Then add other perspectives. See the reaction of the people around you through your own eyes. Hear their congratulations through your own ears. See, hear, and feel the successful task from all angles. Smile.

Finally, burn your own Best Saves DVD. Yours might be called Best Closing Arguments DVD or even Best Sales DVD, but regardless of your profession, at your worst moments, watching this mental program will return you to your focus, eliminate distraction, and deliver you to your peak performance zone. In a way, your mental DVD is a method to programming yourself to this preestablished positive outcome. Program yourself to this outcome, and you will find success.

CLICK! Use Worksheet 13:
My Mental Success DVD to create
your own success programming.

What Now?

If you've followed my advice, you should have overcome at least some of the skepticism you probably felt when we started this chapter. You've probably begun to understand just how powerful your own mind can be as an ally in helping you get what you want. And you may very well have started down the path of imagining your success. The previous two chapters covered how we can really short-circuit ourselves; this one has begun to build the foundations for the positive, proactive new approach I want you to have.

Toolbox Tips

- Work with your skepticism. Listen to it— but challenge it. You decide when to use skepticism; don't let it make the decision.
- Create a tangible picture of your future that incorporates all the successes you want to have.
- Use your senses to reinforce your imagination.
- Write down your dreams.
- Engrain your past successes in your mind at least as deeply as your failures and fears are engrained.

CHAPTER 5

Working Backward

"Know the other, know yourself:
One Hundred challenges without danger;
Know not the other and yet know yourself:
One triumph for one defeat;
Know not the other and know not yourself:
Every challenge is certain peril.
Know Nature and know the Situation:
Triumph completely"
—Sun Tzu

Back once more to Sun Tzu. Do you see a pattern emerging? The highlighted passage here covers what we briefly introduced at the end of the previous chapter. Think about it... how can you possibly succeed in business or in life if you don't know everything you can—what could go right, what could go wrong—about the situations you find yourself in? The answer is you can't. At least not with any consistency. And yet we all do it all the time; we all conduct our daily business without knowing what can go wrong; we all enter business meetings without knowing who and what we're dealing with. And we're still *surprised* when we fail!

In Chapter 4 we started talking a bit about skepticism. I pointed out that it could get in your way of using power visualization to get what you want. Skepticism really is a clear enemy to our progress. If we can go back to the discussion in Chapter 1, skepticism is more like the **fifth obstacle** to a person's success—at least when it comes to any real personal growth.

What am I talking about? And why talk about it now?

Good questions. I bring up skepticism now because what I am about to tell you with the **180 Degree Strategy** involves just that: turning around your mode of thinking—of approaching a problem, of running a business—180 degrees. I'm about to ask you to think in a way completely opposite of what conventional wisdom tells us. So as we learned in the previous chapter, instead of taking the time to present you with a new concept and then spending hours afterwards wondering why you haven't accepted it, I'm going to take care of the obstacles first.

But you'll **never** read these words in this book: "Don't be skeptical."

Why? Because saying "Don't be skeptical," is unrealistic. It's like asking you not to think about an elephant. What did you do just now? You thought about an elephant. So if I begin this chapter as I have by addressing your risk for skepticism, it wouldn't be a good idea to just say "Don't be skeptical." What would happen? You would immediately start to think of all the reasons you *should* be skeptical.

So I'm not going to tell you *not* to be skeptical. In fact, I'm going to *invite it*. What I'm going to tell you is this: Be skeptical, but decide right now *when* you're going to be skeptical.

Whenever you learn new ways of thinking, skepticism is going to show up. For you, it could have happened during Chapter 1. It could have happened while you were reading the last chapter. It could happen six months down the road, when you're already well underway with applying the lessons in this book. The point is that it's *going* to happen.

So before we go one step further with our *Click!* strategies, let's discuss how to identify and control the distraction known as skepticism. This strategy is going to ask you to engage and evaluate your self-talk. In this case, we're going to try to take **negative** self-talk and work to turn it towards a **positive** outcome.

Step One: Ask yourself, *What's wrong with being skeptical?*

Answer: Nothing! Hey, I'm a world-class skeptic myself, so it would be ridiculous for me to tell you that skepticism doesn't have its advantages. It can be a useful tool; you simply need to figure out how and when to apply it.

Step Two: Ask yourself, *When should I engage my skepticism?*

Answer: I can't tell you definitively when you should be skeptical—that's up to you to decide—but let me ask you this: Why would you want to engage your skepticism during a process? What do you gain if you allow your skepticism to get in the way of your learning something new? How much can you get done today, right now, if you spend all your time looking for reasons to be skeptical? Listen to your self-talk. Is skepticism preventing you from real change?

If your answer to that last question is yes, then we need to take a look at our Mind Game Strategies and see if we can figure out a way to take control of skepticism. We need to determine a way to hold off the distraction until later. To that end we need to complete the next two steps in the process.

Step Three: Agree with yourself *that skepticism is okay.*

There's a reason so many people are prone to this common obstacle. It's okay. It's worked for you in the past, hasn't it? It's prevented you from trying a whole range of things that would have been a waste of time. So tell yourself it's fine to be skeptical. No matter what I or anybody else tells you, you're simply not going to be able to give up skepticism. You can't just make it go away. And you don't want it to go away anyway—it's too useful. Embrace that idea.

Step Four: Pick a time and place when you promise yourself you will be allowed to stop everything and review it skeptically.

What do I mean by that? I mean pick a time—tonight, tomorrow, six months from now, whenever—when you will allow yourself to be skeptical about everything you have read (and hopefully tried) today and in the future.

And I mean this very literally. Take a look at your calendar for the week. Let's say you plan on being finished with this chapter before work today. Now look at today's listings on your calendar and pick the first gap you have between meetings or obligations. Let's say it's between 4:00 and 4:10 p.m. Take that very specific time to skeptically review the material you're about to learn.

By the way, I'd be out of bounds if I told you that this technique worked only for the learning you're about to do in this chapter. If you make an agreement with yourself—much like you did with the Trunk Card in Chapter Three—and you keep that agreement, you will find success in controlling this common distraction.

So plan to be skeptical at 4:00 p.m. And then, today, start

putting into practice the material you'll learn in the coming pages.

Now just because you do this doesn't mean you will be immune to skepticism today. There's still one more step.

Step Five: Listen to your self-talk as you put this plan to action.

The instant you notice yourself being skeptical, snap your fingers, *Click!* and say "four p.m…four p.m…four p.m." Watch how quickly the distraction of skepticism loses power.

But here's the clincher: since you've promised yourself you will be skeptical at 4:00 p.m., you **must** stop at 4:00 p.m. and be skeptical. Even if you find during the day that the 180 Degree Strategy works better than you would have thought—and I'm confident if you give it a chance it will—you must keep your meeting with yourself. Do this, and you will be able to move forward with a clear head and a greater understanding of the concept as a whole. You will find yourself reaching more-favorable outcomes.

So what do you do during your 4:00 skepticism meeting? You talk about the 180 Degree Strategy (or any other strategy or concept you feel a little skeptical about) with yourself. I have and will continue to discuss the concept of "talking with yourself" throughout this book, but let me give you a little refresher on how to do that here:

- Have a dialogue with yourself.
- Discuss everything that may be causing your skepticism and why.
- Discuss what worked during the day and what didn't.
- Determine whether continued skepticism would be beneficial to your continued growth.

Now let me offer a quick tip. When you're talking with your-self, don't move your lips. You'll look strange if you're literally talking to yourself in public. Keep the dialogue internal and you'll find this process benefits the goal of improving your self-talk and making it less negative as well.

Rethinking Your Business

With the strategies on how to manage skepticism out of the way, we can now turn to the reasons I brought it up in the first place. We can now begin learning how to approach your busi-ness and your life from the opposite direction. We can begin figuring out ways to work backward to a solution.

Common sense would dictate that we begin at the begin-ning and try to figure out the best ways to meet a desired resolution. But with *Click!* we're using an **outcome-based** thought process, so the most logical place to begin is actually at the end.

What? You might be asking yourself. Conventional wisdom likely suggests that you've never done this sort of thing before. To that I can say only this: Exactly.

In this chapter we're going to shift conventional wisdom and begin to look at outcomes first, obstacles second, and solu-tions last—rather than the other way around. We're going to turn things around 180 degrees. But first we must reevaluate exactly what it is we hope to turn around.

What do you need right now? Forget about the past, the future, hypotheticals, whatever. Before we can flip the whole process backward, we need to figure out the axis point. We need to figure out where you, your business, your clients, and your competition stand. Remember, it may take eight or ten plays to score a touchdown, but you can complete only one play at a time! If you don't know what you need right now, you'll find yourself missing all kinds of present-day opportunities.

For example, I had a client who owned a small business that constantly seemed to be struggling with cash flow. His first and only perceived solution to that problem was that he needed to get his employees to generate more business. So he and I did a SWOT (Strengths-Weaknesses-Opportunities-Threats) analysis on him, his company, his employees, and his target clients. What we found surprised us. What we found was that, then and there, as we spoke, his company was bringing in more business than the owner knew what to do with. He just didn't realize it because he didn't have the staff in place to process it all so he could complete it—and get paid.

Because this client of mine hadn't been taking the time to figure out what he needed right now, he had missed all those opportunities to achieve his goals.

It's a more common issue than you might think. Before we begin with 180 Degree material, do your own **SWOT Analysis**. SWOT stands for Strengths-Weaknesses-Opportunities-Threats. I don't love the word "weakness" because I view it as simply an opportunity to grow, but this is a classic. Turn to Worksheet 15 right now and follow the directions.

CLICK! Use Worksheet 15:
My SWOT Analysis to identify the strengths
you bring to the table, areas where you could
improve, opportunities that are open to you,
and threats that confront you.

Why is it important to size up your real present situation like this? Try this one:

The owner of an M&A firm had a client who thought he wanted to sell his manufacturing business after twenty-five years. It had taken a good portion of this man's life to build the firm from the ground up and bring it to the point of its current profitability. He loved what he had created over the years, but he thought perhaps it was time to get out and retire.

My client—the M&A guy—put everything in place. He found an English firm that wanted to buy. They sent people over to run the numbers, kick the tires, etc. The money, the sale terms, and the interest rates were all lined up, and the sale appeared certain to go smoothly. On the day of the closing, however, the business owner decided not to sell. He said he couldn't imagine turning over his clients to "those people."

My client was in shock; he had done everything he could have imagined to make the sale happen, but something simply wasn't working. What could possibly have gone wrong? As I determined, it was a matter of perspective. He wasn't thinking about this sale in the right way.

"What was being sold?" I asked him.

"A manufacturing business," he said.

Not exactly. What the business owner was selling had taken him twenty-five years to build. He had spent all his time nurturing it. Feeding it. Watching it grow. He probably spent many nights awake with it when it was sick. If he could have, he probably would have even changed its diaper. What the guy was selling wasn't a business—it was as if he were selling his child.

Neither the M&A firm nor the prospective buyers had taken that into account. They treated the sale as if it were a straightforward business transaction. They followed the usual steps to complete the sale without any reference to the prospective seller's personal investment in his manufacturing business. They were thinking about things in the wrong way.

No matter what kind of situation you are in, there are always some invisible dynamics at work. Sometimes a simple SWOT Analysis can point out what could go wrong. In this case it would have helped the M&A firm discover that the business owner might not have been quite ready to get completely out—and certainly wasn't ready to sell his child to just anyone. It would have given the M&A firm a chance to take a completely different approach. Instead, they had to start over from square one.

Let's now turn our attention to a couple of strategies designed to help you avoid this kind of situation.

The 180 Degree Strategy

As the M&A firm owner discovered, it's easier to stay out of trouble than to get out of trouble. If he had approached the sale with the right mindset, he never would have lost the deal. Instead, he had to spend time and effort on trying to get his potential buyer to come back to the table to renegotiate.

So if we're going to stay out of trouble instead of spending all our time fixing and fighting against trouble, we have to approach things completely differently.

When you are business leader, conventional wisdom dictates that you outline your instructions, your how-to, and then send somebody to implement or execute the plan. But there is another strategy, drawn from our reverse mentality. If we take that strategy one step further, we can help identify places where individuals, teams, and even whole companies tend to drop the ball. Without this strategy you could end up like the M&A firm owner. The results could be catastrophic. Millions could be squandered, and business could be lost.

Do me a favor. Reach into your toolbox and pull out that Magic Wand we talked about in Chapter 4. Give it a flick and take yourself to the year 20XX (five years from today). Ideally, you and your company are more successful now than you were all the way back then, but let's not think about that right now. Instead, let's take the time to fill out a list.

Sit down…grab a pen and paper…and create a list of anything and everything you could do to @#$% up your company.

For the record, "@#$%" is a medical term; replace it with the words "screw up" if you like. Create a list of anything and everything you could do to screw up your company in the short term. What would it take to make sure that, if you yourself were standing in 20XX, your company would be in complete ruin?

Do you have a business partner? A team member? A superior at work? If you do, have him, her, or them complete this project too.

Number your list from one to four, one to twenty, one to fifty, whatever. Fill in as many **mistakes** you could make or **obstacles** you could fail to surmount between now and 20XX. Be creative. There are thousands of ways to destroy a company.

When you're finished, **evaluate your list**. Then compare your list to the list of anyone else in your circle you have asked to complete the exercise as well. If you have twenty-two ways to screw up your company and your colleague has four, then it's time the two of you had a discussion. If you have two ways and your colleague has a completely different two, then it's time the two of you had a discussion.

Start to create a composite list. Include your screwups, your colleagues' screwups, your superiors' screwups. If you're a business owner, ask everybody in the firm what he or she could do to @#$% up the company.

A member of the sales team might say, "Well, I could quit picking up the phone."

Your receptionist could tell you, "I could be nasty to everyone…I could keep people on hold for an hour."

The maintenance staff could come up with, "We could sit in the break room all day and leave the lobby a mess."

Take it all down; compile the list. What you should have when you're finished is a list of dozens, maybe even hundreds of things you and your coworkers, employees, and superiors could do to ensure your company fails to succeed in the future.

CLICK! Use Worksheet 16:
My @#$% List to look at your business
from the other side.

Now **post that list**. From this point forward, all the people in your company know what they **cannot** do if they hope to succeed. Everyone in the company knows the obstacles to success in your business.

This process might seem strange, but again, refrain from being skeptical. Revisit your skepticism a few days later. Let it all play out. And if you have time between now and then, give the 180 Degree Strategy a try. You'll be shocked at the results.

Why is this so effective? Because once you know the

problems you will encounter, the mistakes you can make—once you literally have them written down and staring you in the face—you will be able to rest easy, knowing that you and your employees, coworkers, and superiors are well aware of how to avoid screwups. You'll move in to what I like to call the Ambien/Lunestra Zone: you'll be able to sleep better at night.

You won't spend any more time silently worrying about what could go wrong because you'll already know what could go wrong. You will have a better understanding of the thought processes and fears of the people with whom you work. And you will know exactly where in your company you need to intervene.

Skilled football players spend hours each week learning how to avoid problems before they arise. Running backs work on taking care of the football so they don't fumble. Wide receivers learn how to tuck the ball before the collision. Quarterbacks repeat throws and study reads constantly in the hopes of improving accuracy and decision making, and as a result, cutting down on turnovers.

Complete the steps of the 180 Degree Strategy and you will be practicing in much the same way. You will know your obstacles and potential problems **in advance** and, as a result, be able to **avoid them entirely**.

So let's take our lessons from the previous chapter and combine them with this one, shall we?

To get your team—including yourself—to work with you, you need to ask yourself three questions:

1. What's my strategy for [this task]?
2. Is there anything I can think of that would get in the way of my getting the outcome I want?

3. What do I need to provide for things to go
   well?

Let's take the three questions from a 180 Degree Strategy perspective. Now we're standing in 20XX (or five years from whenever you are reading this book). Look backward to today. Those questions now become a bit more complex and powerful. They might look more like this:

1. Give me three things you don't want to have
   happen.
2. Describe the most embarrassing thing that
   could happen.
3. List three things about your job, project, or
   business that keep you up at night.
4. Identify the things that could cause your
   presentation, project, negotiation, or
   performance to falter.

Ask yourself and your colleagues these questions and you will often find yourself saying, "Thank God I did that." Why? Because more often than not you will discover that your coworker/employee/superior—individuals who otherwise always seem prepared—are as close to prepared as you would like them to be. People get so caught up in what they are doing that they lose sight of why they are doing it. Also, as we've seen, although we know everything we can do to screw things up, we don't always keep those things in mind as we go about our daily lives.

Five Years Out

Over the years my clients have had a huge amount of success using the Magic Wand approach. They simply envision—in great detail—everything they want to be part of their lives five years from now and work backward. You may already have filled in Worksheet 9: My Magic Wand of 20XX. I want you to take it out again and have a slightly different look at it, one that integrates a number of the strategies we have been discussing so far. I gave you some good general questions, but for this to really work you have to be as specific as possible. Let's start with a particular aspect of your life. Since we've been talking about business in this chapter, maybe that's the best place to begin. What matters to you most in business?

- The people who work with you?
- The specific tasks you are charged with?
- How much money you make?
- Where the office is located?
- What it looks like?
- What you wear to work?
- The successes you enjoy every day (cases won if you're a litigator, goals prevented if you're a goaltender, etc.)?

As we've seen, for things to work out the way you want them to, you will probably encounter some obstacles—and you'll have to persist through them. You'll also find that you get in your own way and screw things up; that's okay; we all do. But—and this is equally important—you'll enjoy some intermediate successes along the way. Stand at that point five years from now... and visualize it all.

CLICK! Use Worksheet 21:
My Integrated Working Backward
Strategy to document where you want
to be and all the things you will have to
accomplish along the way.

What Now?

If you did all the exercises in this chapter, you've done a lot of work. You started by figuring out where you really are right now. Then you listed everything you can do to screw up your goals. Finally, you didn't just look at your future; you actually visited it. You should have a very good sense of how the *Click!* system works—and how you can use it to your advantage. Contrary to what many of us have been told, daydreaming can pay off. In the next chapter, we'll build on this even further by exploring the idea that no matter what you're trying to do, you are the CEO of your own company: You, Inc.

Toolbox Tips

- Always know where you stand at a given moment. A quick SWOT Analysis can give you an invaluable snapshot.
- Be aware that there are any number of ways you can screw up, but if you take the time to list them, they are less likely to occur.
- Look at things from the other side—as if they have already happened.

CHAPTER 6

You, Inc.

"Know the other, know yourself:
One Hundred challenges without danger;
*Know not the other and yet **know yourself**:*
One triumph for one defeat;
Know not the other and know not yourself:
Every challenge is certain peril.
Know Nature and know the Situation:
Triumph completely"
—Sun Tzu

Throughout this book so far I've asked you to look at this quote from Sun Tzu, to take it in, and to use it almost as a mantra. You've probably gotten so used to it that you've started skimming over it. Right now, before we go on, take a moment to read it again.

I want you to consider what would happen if you looked at yourself differently. Look at the present—the "right now" of who you are. Get the picture clear in your mind. Now imagine you the observer floating up and away from you the reality. You are getting farther and farther from yourself until you are finally about 1,000 feet away.

Imagine…that you could look down and see not only what's going on in your mind but also the situations in your life playing themselves out as well as the people in your life interacting with you.

Can you **see yourself**? How would you **define yourself**?

You may come up with any number of words to describe what you see and feel, but I'm going to suggest right here and now that realigning your thinking will benefit you in the long run. If you're an accountant, do you see simply an accountant? If you're an entrepreneur, do you see simply an entrepreneur? If you're a receptionist, do you see simply a receptionist? Well, if you do, let's see if we can change that.

What if I said to you that the person you are looking down on right now—you—is the CEO of his or her own company? What would change about your life if you saw yourself in this way? Would you work harder? Would you take more responsibility for your actions? Would you get better results on a daily basis? Would your professional life seem more significant?

Now…see yourself in this way.

Imagine…that you are the CEO of your own company. You, Inc.

Having trouble? Then let's try another visualization.

Look down upon yourself seated at a desk on which rests a small, stapled stack of papers. You grip a silver pen and are readying to sign on the dotted line at the bottom of the page you just read. It is a contract you are looking down upon—and it is the most important one you will ever sign.

It happens very quickly, particularly if you are a professional athlete. The contract is in front of you, your pen moves across the paper, the ink is not yet dry, and your business status changes immediately. Instantly, according to the contract, you have become the **CEO of your own company**.

From now on, every decision you make, both inside and out of the office, on and off the field, becomes a **business** decision. It is no longer just the company or the franchise. It is no longer the sales department or the football team. **You** are the franchise... You are the business leader... You are the product... You are the talent. However you want to look at it, the most important opinion is yours, and the most important decisions are the ones *you* make in order to benefit *your* company—*you*.

Got that? Can you visualize it? So how does this **change** anything?

Like this:

If you walk in to companies to do business, tell me you wouldn't enjoy dealing with people who thought of themselves as CEOs of their own company. Wouldn't they be more responsible for providing you with the best-quality information and service? Wouldn't they care more about your needs as a customer?

Certainly changes the motivation, doesn't it?

Successful CEOs are constantly challenged to guide their companies towards long-term success. Focusing on their product or service, they become responsible for (and experts in) a whole range of things—from product development and improvement to public relations to sales and marketing to branding to any financial and legal issues that may affect the firm. And success, once reached, requires constant attention. This is simply because, as a CEO, taking your eye off the ball can lead to disaster.

If you began to **focus** on these things...if you began to **work towards learning** how to meet head-on any challenges you might face during the work day...if you **took the time** and energy to solve any of your company's problems on your own, what would that do to your business status? How would that improve your status as an employee? How would that improve the quality of your work life?

The short answer is this: the possibilities for your future would be *boundless.*

For the sake of argument, let's say you buy into this concept. You are the business. You are the CEO of You, Inc. Ask yourself, *What am I going to do* differently *now that I am CEO of my own company? What am I going to do today that I didn't do yesterday?*

The possibilities are endless. And so are the results.

Here are just a few of them:

1. If you think of yourself as the CEO of your own company, you will find yourself consistently reviewing your **existing strengths**, identifying **new strengths**, and **building confidence** that will **enhance your ability to move forward**.

    Potential obstacle: you will need to begin to *compliment yourself* regularly…not easy for most of us to do since we were told as kids to avoid it.

    Important tip: *get over it.* Remember, as the CEO of You, Inc., you are in charge of a very small company—just you—and you are therefore responsible for everything it takes to improve that company's status.

2. If you think of yourself as the CEO of your own company…*you* are in charge of continuing education. You are no longer

spending time in company-provided training or coaching programs simply because they are required. Now you will think as though you are adding this free training to your toolbox. From now on you are not just sitting silently through training; you are picking the brains of every experienced person you can find in the hopes of adding to the resources of You, Inc.

3. This is truly a win-win scenario. Or even win-win-win. If you take greater responsibility for expanding your knowledge about your product, service, or role, your company wins and so do you. And the third winner is the customer.

4. If you think of yourself as the CEO of your own company...you can, if you choose, begin to take a broader view of your field.

5. In other words, you become a student of the challenges faced by your company and your existing clients (and their challenges). You will find yourself **asking** more questions and **listening** more—not because it's the job, but because you *can*. And also because you *want to*.

6. If you think of yourself as the CEO of your own company...you will seek to learn as much as possible every day.

7. When you take responsibility for You, Inc., the search for knowledge becomes much

more **personal** and **urgent**. You will find yourself striving to see how many problems you can solve before heading home from work. You will find yourself striving to see how many business relationships you can build in a day or a week. Once again, who wins? Everyone.

8. If you think of yourself as the CEO of your own company...you are in charge of marketing.

9. How would you market yourself? How would you market You, Inc.? We'll learn a little more about what other people are doing in the pages to follow.

Don't Go It Alone

There is one fundamental flaw to this You, Inc. strategy. In confidence, most CEOs would tell you that sometimes they feel as though they are **alone at the top**. Being the kind of person who feels directly responsible for *all* struggles and *all* successes tends to lead to a rather solitary lifestyle. If you're the expert in everything, who can you trust but yourself? And when your expertise falls short, to whom do you turn for answers?

Yes, even CEOs sometimes need answers. Although it sometimes may feel like everyone expects them to have all the answers, good CEOs know they simply don't—nor do they need to. What they *do* need is three things: the right questions, the right people to ask, and the courage and confidence to ask. Also, this must be in complete confidence. Sometimes people really get a lot of value from having a designated confidential sounding board.

Smart people surround themselves with smart people; that's what makes them smart people.

A good CEO needs a good team. No CEO can expect to move a product without a capable sales team. No sane quarterback would face a defensive line with only the center to protect him. You really don't want to be sacked in football or in business.

So if you are going to think of yourself as CEO of You, Inc., you must make the decision to understand that you cannot expect to go it alone. There will be some problems you simply cannot solve on your own. There will be some problems that are better met with the expertise of an outside source. There will be some projects that will be completed quicker and better if you have the help of a team.

In order to eliminate the central flaw to this comprehensive strategy, you must begin to think of yourself not just as CEO of an individual person but as CEO of a team of individuals who can **meet the needs of anyone at any time.** Seem like a tall order? It doesn't have to be.

The first step towards building your team is to determine what needs your company has to fill. What is it you can't do on your own? Where does your knowledge or expertise fall short? What kinds of people would help round out You, Inc. and make it the kind of **powerhouse company** every CEO would dream to lead?

SWOT Analysis (Revisited)

This would be a good time for you to complete another SWOT Analysis. Not many businesspeople or athletes consider the concept of team building after all. Make no mistake, whether you have experience with assembling a team or not, **knowing**

yourself better is the best way towards understanding what You, Inc. will need.

CLICK! Worksheet 15: My SWOT Analysis will help organize your thoughts as you do this exercise.

Strengths:

1. What talents have taken you to where you are professionally?
2. What do you do really well?

Weaknesses (Again, I don't like the word "weakness," but it fits as the "W" in SWOT):

1. What areas do you need to develop or identify (so you can hire people who have that particular skill set)?
2. In which areas do you need assistance in order to maintain and assure your professional or personal growth?
3. How do you protect your future? (You dream the future and look backward, avoiding things that might get in the way or derail you.)

CLICK! Worksheet 9:
My Magic Wand of 20XX will help you
envision the future you really want.

Opportunities... What opportunities are open to you today that you are not taking advantage of both in and out of the office, on and off the field?

Being a CEO, you are required to look beyond the here and now as well. For every decision you make regarding an opportunity, you must look ahead, well beyond your time in that corner office or leading that franchise, to determine how your decisions and actions will affect your company's future. That notion leads to a couple of important questions:

1. **Question**... Am I looking far enough into the future? (With every decision, many CEOs are looking to 20XX and working backward.)
2. **Question**... Is my lifestyle a risk to my company, its image, or its future earnings potential?
3. **Question**... Am I or my product/service commercial or endorsement material?
4. **Also, really look around**—including behind you:
5. **Question**... What opportunities are past and cannot be recovered?
6. **Question**... What opportunities are past but could possibly be brought back to life?

7. **Question**… What opportunities are right in front of you?

8. **Question**… What opportunities can you see on the way?

Threats… What threats exist for your company? Some possibilities include:

1. Letting someone else control your company.
2. Asking the wrong people the wrong questions.
3. Not seeking second opinions.
4. Inaction.

Now that you understand yourself and, most important, the areas where things could be improved or that represent the greatest danger to You, Inc., you need to begin to think about a few strategies to help get your company moving in the right direction. As I have mentioned, CEOs don't survive if they try to do everything on their own. They each need a team, and in just a moment we're going to learn how to assemble and start thinking about that team.

You must begin to think about your company's future. What are the best ways for you to advance yourself and your company's success? Whom should you turn to in order to ensure continuous growth? Whom should you turn to if a problem surfaces? By the time this chapter is through, you will have learned a strategy on how to find answers to all of these questions.

But first, it will be important for you, the CEO, to learn how to **market yourself** and the company you now lead. The best way to do that is to quit thinking about how you're going to sell your product or service and start thinking about how you can resolve problems your prospective clients face.

Strategy #1: I Sell Mistakes

Most of us realize that others' perceptions of us cover only a small part of who we are and what we are capable of. In other words, most people recognize that they are **typecast**. Being typecast by someone else's perception of what you do creates a range of significant problems, but let's examine only a few.

For one thing, everybody knows exactly what your job is all about. Or at least everybody thinks he or she does. You are *defined by your profession.* If you allow your profession to offer the first and most complete definition of you, you lose the opportunity to show you are different from everyone else and think differently as well. What's worse, you miss opportunities to **make connections** because discussions with potential colleagues are shut down almost immediately.

If you let your profession define you, this is how the discussion will typically go:

"What do you do?" someone will ask.

"I'm a CPA," you'll reply.

Okay, that person will think. *I know exactly what this guy does. Let's move on…*

So if Bill Jones is a CPA, he has a card that reads "CPA." He hands it over to people willing to extend a hand for it. But as soon as they take the card and read Bill's title, their eyes glaze over…they don't care anymore about what Bill has to say about his job or how he might help them. They *already know* what he does, or at least someone who does what he does. Bill is dropped quickly into the CPA category… Discussion over.

If this person whose eyes have just glazed over is a

prospective client, Bill has already failed to meet a few challenges. In the six seconds Bill had to make himself seem interesting enough to hold the prospect's interest, he knew he had to:

- Convince the prospect to offer to buy his product or service on the spot—no questions asked. (Bill knows this isn't likely, but we all can dream.)
  or
- Show the prospect exactly what he does and what his value can be to the client immediately. (Again, not likely).
  or
- Demonstrate to the prospect that he might be someone he or she would like to call in the future.
  or
- Quickly show that he isn't just like every other CPA this prospect has ever met.

But Bill, in saying, "I'm a CPA," failed to accomplish any of these tasks *instantaneously.*

So now what?

Well, in the scenario above, Bill probably has about ten more seconds to do or say something that will break the dreaded "glazeover." What he needs to do in that time is seem *different* and *compelling.* And the best way to do that is to say something completely unusual.

I have met thousands of people in business and social settings who have explained what they do, and in my estimation there is one clear winner of the "most unique introduction" derby. At a very large networking event, I was standing with some friends, lawyers, accountants, and asset managers when an attractive woman walked into the center of the group.

Naturally, we asked her what she did.

She took her business card out of her pocket, held it up with the blank side facing us, and said, "Men are interested in two things: sex and money." She hesitated a second, flipped her card over, and revealed that it pictured the dollar sign logo of her venture capital firm. Then she said, "I take care of the money."

Needless to say, we all laughed hysterically. I guarantee that no one in the group will forget her.

Fortunately, there are less-dramatic ways to approach this challenge and still see results. We'll get into a more comprehensive approach later, but for now we'll cover the quickest way to spark a meaningful business conversation.

Wherever you are…whether it's a networking event, a business meeting, a social environment, or the proverbial elevator meeting, you will want to be prepared to make the best use of the **six seconds** you have to become different.

Let's try the question on Bill one more time. Imagine that you walk up to Bill during a networking meeting and ask, "So what do you do?"

Imagine that this time Bill pauses a bit and replies with a smile, "Well… I sell mistakes."

We'll get into what this means in just a moment, but for now let's ask ourselves these questions. You just heard Bill say he sells mistakes for a living.

1. Does Bill have your attention?
2. Does Bill sound like everyone else?
3. Would you walk away from Bill?

4. Would you *truly* want to learn more about what Bill does for a living?
5. Would you think about the mistakes you yourself are making?
6. Would you think about the mistakes your own company is making?
7. What would be your response to this question?

The answers are simple. Of course Bill would have your attention. You've never heard anything like what Bill just said. And it's so cryptic! "I sell mistakes!" What does that mean?

Naturally, your curiosity will be piqued. Bill will have successfully used that first six seconds to overcome some of the major challenges in networking communication.

"What does that mean?" you'll ask him with a smile.

"Well," Bill would say, "let's fast forward for a minute and think about what your business will be like in ten months. Say you've got an issue—a big issue—that could lead to your company losing ground on the competition. What would that issue be?"

You might shake your head in confusion.

"Let me put it to you another way," Bill would say. "Imagine you are going to drive across the country. You punch the coordinates into your GPS, and it gives you detailed, step-by-step directions. What's missing from those directions, though, is important information about speed traps and traffic cams. Now imagine your GPS can actually provide you with that information. Would that be something that might help you?"

This would be the point when you think about the biggest professional disaster you can imagine. After a few moments you would relate that disaster to Bill.

"What if I told you..." Bill would say, pausing for effect. "What if I told you I've worked with people who have made that same mistake? What if I told you I've helped people overcome that same mistake? What if I told you I could help you avoid that mistake? What would that be worth to you and your company?"

These kinds of questions are likely to be met with eager responses on your part. After all, what if you could tell your next prospect that investing in your company now could save millions down the road? Would it be easier for you to make a sale? Of course it would.

Many skeptics roll their eyes at this concept, but let them roll. The rolling stops the minute they see this working.

And selling mistakes is simply one concept. The point here is that too many people, when presented with a business opportunity, simply try to sell their companies' products or services through traditional means. In other words, everybody uses the exact same tools to get the message across. Everybody has business cards. Everybody has flashy handouts. Everybody has company-prescribed gimmicks. But few people take the opportunity to listen to what a prospect wants and communicate their desire and ability to meet those wants.

So, as CEO of You, Inc., how *do* you develop the ability to meet those wants?

CLICK! Worksheet 18: Mistakes
provides a straightforward way to think
about how you can sell mistakes.

Strategy #2: The 20XX Silos

Life isn't just business. You may have children who need to get to football practice. You may have a spouse who needs help cooking dinner. You may aspire to learn how to play the guitar. And obviously you want to meet people and take opportunities to advance your career. These are all very valid and important elements of your life. But they all pull you in a dozen different directions. Many of them cause you to lose focus on the most important things in your life—which causes those important things to remain untended. What we're talking about is work/life balance. It's a critical factor for most people in business today.

What if we could separate all of them? What if you could divide your life into categories or silos that hold every dream and desire you possess? And what if you could use your silos to plan how your life will be over the next five years—into the year 20XX?

Today, I have many clients doing exactly that.

So how does it work?

First, you separate your needs into three silos: **Professional**, **Personal**, and **Family**. There can be more or fewer categories if you like, but these three tend to serve as a good start. Second, you get three sheets of paper and label one "Professional," one "Personal," and so on. If you are artistically inclined, you can even draw a silo on each sheet.

What you will be doing is hanging your silos up on a wall, by the mirror, at your office, wherever you might see them on a daily basis. They are going to be the guides to shaping your present and future life—and you will get so used to seeing them that they will eventually become a part of your subconscious.

Now before skepticism takes over, let me tell you that this exercise *really does work.*

The **Professional Silo** can be used as a visual guide for exactly how you are building You, Inc. What you will place in this silo are people and opportunities that can help you achieve all those professional elements you cannot achieve alone. Every time you are handed a business card and make a connection with a potential partner, when you get home (or back to work), take that business card and tape or tack it to your Professional Silo.

By 20XX, your Professional Silo will likely be full of business cards, and you'll have made so many professional contacts and sources for referral that there won't be a single business need that you, the CEO of You, Inc., cannot meet. You won't find a single prospective client who could not benefit from a professional relationship with you.

In other words, regardless of what you do, you will begin to see a kind of **consulting practice** evolve right before your eyes. You do not need to quit your job and start your own literal company in order to take advantage of this consulting practice. The people and opportunities listed in your Professional Silo merely represent your ability to go above and beyond the call of your job. They represent your ability to get *anything* done. They can also become a personal safety net.

Once you have your network in place, you will begin to think of yourself not just as a CEO but as a group—which as we will see is an even more powerful way of thinking. This is because, as a CEO, there are occasionally problems you cannot solve alone. As a group, there is no problem you cannot solve without picking up the phone and calling one of the experts you have aligned yourself with in the silo.

CLICK! Worksheet 17:
*You, Inc. Resources can help you figure
out what resources you will need as head
of your own firm.*

Strategy #3: The Jones Group

Do me a favor and enter your last name in the following blank:

The _____ Group

From now on, for our purposes, this is the name of your company. Let's assume your name is Jones. So your company is called "The Jones Group."

Now we know that you have been looking at things from 1,000 feet above. If you have been thinking of yourself as a CEO and letting people know you sell mistakes, you have started to accumulate information about the challenges your clients and non-clients face. You must now use that information to determine the best way to help your clients and non-clients meet those challenges.

Why? you might ask. Because helping people meet their challenges is the **best way to build business relationships**— ones that will inevitably lead to better sales, quicker career advancement, and more personal and professional options for you to choose from.

In the time you have been working and networking, building your silos, you have likely discovered what other professionals do and the solutions they provide. What if you could

harness those abilities? What if you could use those other professionals you have placed in your career silo to **boost the capabilities** of the Jones Group?

Imagine that you are an accountant. Now imagine that you meet a person seeking the services of a financial planner. Can you offer those services alone? No…not likely. But if you, the problem-solving CEO, had the business card of a financial planner in your career silo, what would that do for the Jones Group? How would your company benefit from being able to offer solutions you cannot offer on your own?

If you knew a financial planner from your career silo and had decided to bring him or her in to the Jones Group, you would have been able to address a need you would not have otherwise been able to address. A prospective customer who would have otherwise ignored everything you had to say about your job or the products you offer might have perked up to hear that you could *help* him or her.

See? You weren't just trying to force-feed your accounting services to a person seeking financial advice. With your career silo and your Jones Group understanding, you were able to solve a problem the prospective customer was *asking you* to solve. And to whom is that prospective customer going to turn someday when he or she *does* have accounting needs? The Jones Group, of course. And as for the financial planner you sent that prospective customer to, to whom is he or she going to refer all of his or her accounting business? The Jones Group, of course.

Now, with that thought in mind, look at what you have at hand as the Jones Group: a huge consulting company without the headaches of overhead and with the potential to solve almost any problem your clients present with just one phone call. Suddenly you become much more than what the person

initially perceives. You are no longer just an insurance agent—
a person useful only to the customer seeking insurance. You
become a CEO...a specialist...a *team*. You and the Jones
Group can meet *any* need.

The Jones Group. Has a nice ring to it, doesn't it?

So the next step in this Jones Group paradigm is to **continue to build your team**. If you don't have a financial planner
in your Professional Silo, it's time to meet one. If you don't
know an accountant, find one you can trust.

But more than that, you must start to understand there is
almost no one you meet who can't serve the Jones Group in
some way. Know a sports agent? She might come in handy.
Know someone who ghostwrites books? He might be able to
serve the Jones Group as well. Each person you meet in a business (or even personal) setting has unique talents that could
one day assist you in solving problems for your existing and
prospective clients. These people are likely to become friends
beyond your initial expectations—and they are all likely to
benefit from their participation in your powerhouse new
company.

CLICK! Worksheet 2:
*My Professional Silo will help you organize
the information you gather from others and
add them to the silo of Jones, Inc.*

Where to Start

Let's say you buy in to this concept. Let's say you're all about
becoming The [Your Last Name] Group and thinking of

yourself as its CEO. You now need to make that group a reality. Where do you start?

Well, the steps are really quite simple:

1. Get to know yourself as The [Your Last Name] Group.
2. Go to www.networksolutions.com (or another URL-providing site) and reserve a .com name for yourself (i.e., www. thejonesgroup.com).
3. Once you have your domain name, visit www.vistaprint.com, where you can get your hands on 250 free business cards that carry the name of your group, the services you provide, your URL address, and your email address (i.e., The Jones Group, Business Solutions, www.thejonesgroup. com, bill@thejonesgroup.com).

Now you have printed affirmation that you are in business for yourself. Has anything changed? Not really… You have always been responsible for who you are and how you behave. All that has come of this is a change in perspective—and many times, perspective is the most important thing in business.

You don't even have to give this card out to anyone. Put one up on your bathroom mirror at home, one in your Professional Silo, one in your home office, and one in your wallet. It will keep your mind thinking differently. It will get you visualizing that you are not just a seller of a product or service, you are the CEO of a high-powered group that can meet *any* professional customer need.

But don't take my word for it. I had just finished presenting this You, Inc. concept at the Goaltending Consultant Group

Prospect Camp, which plays host to some of the hottest hockey goalie prospects in the country. In a six-year period it has led to the development of an unbelievable twenty-two NHL draft picks. Because it was such a valuable camp, as you can imagine, my speech was featured right up alongside those of NHL head coaches, goalies, US National Team players and coaches, and other hockey legends.

When I finished presenting this well-received speech, I was approached by Brian Daccord, CEO of Stop It Goaltending and the Goaltender Consulting Group. Brian related his own story about how powerful this business card strategy—and the visualization that comes along with it—can be. Here's what he told me:

"I'm a big believer in writing things down. I've accomplished almost everything I've written down."

"It really is powerful," I said earnestly.

Brian explained just how true that statement was. About five years prior, he was finishing up his career as a hockey goalie in Europe. He had always known that once he retired he wanted to land the job of goalie coach with the Boston Bruins, the team he had watched religiously while growing up in Montreal. His conviction to this dream was made stronger when he went to school in Boston some years later.

But there was one problem with this dream. He had no NHL playing or coaching experience—and if you look across the NHL, there is almost no one in a coaching position without prior experience with professional hockey in North America.

Determined, Brian went to a machine he had seen and paid a few dollars to have 100 business cards printed that read:

Brian Daccord
Assistant Coach, Boston Bruins

He didn't know the address of the organization or the phone number, so he made some up.

"I wound up throwing ninety-nine of them away and stuck only one in my wallet," Brian told me. "But I saw that card every time I opened my wallet. Five years after I printed the cards, I was hired by the Bruins."

Imagine the power of that story. The chances of Brian making it into the fold as an NHL coach were extremely slim. He had never played or coached in the NHL before. He had no NHL ties whatsoever. But he saw his dream, wrote it down on a business card, and subconsciously made it happen.

Get the cards… **Imagine**…and you may be surprised.

CLICK! Use Worksheet 19:
My Ideal Business Card to help you visualize
where you want your career to go.

What Now?

Imagine…for a moment…that you no longer have to feel defined by what you do for a living.

Imagine…for a moment…that you are responsible for everything your company does.

Imagine…for a moment…that you have a team of individuals working for and with you every day.

Imagine…for a moment…that you can provide solutions *every* consumer is seeking.

Imagine…for a moment…that there is no problem you cannot solve.

The beauty of the You, Inc. model of thinking is that all of these things come true. Clients of mine have seen remarkable improvement in their management, sales, and executive teams. And this works globally; it's as true in Singapore as it is in San Francisco.

When you picture yourself as the CEO of your own company, you begin to take more responsibility for the things that crop up in your everyday, professional life. You will find yourself working hard to absorb as much information as you can. You will find yourself learning new jobs even when you aren't asked to do so. You will find yourself solving more problems inside and out of work.

With the I Sell Mistakes and Jones Group strategies, you will meet more people, gain more clients, get more referrals, and enjoy more meaningful business conversations.

But the best part about these You, Inc. strategies is that they will get you away from feeling defined by what you do. You can continue to do your job—absolutely—but what you will find is that taking greater responsibility, building your own team, and developing business contacts will help you do that job better.

And, hey, if you ever decide to go off on your own, you will have an amazing consulting group already prepared.

Toolbox Tips

- Look for ways to redefine yourself as a bigger entity.
- Remain aware of what the bigger entity would do differently than you as an individual.
- Understand what you do well—and where you need help.
- Assemble resources to help you function as a larger entity.
- Help others see you as a bigger entity by talking about your work in surprising—and relevant—ways.
- Write down your bigger vision.

CHAPTER 7

Your Competitive Edge

"Know the other, know yourself:
One Hundred challenges without danger;
Know not the other and yet know yourself:
One triumph for one defeat;
Know not the other and know not yourself:
Every challenge is certain peril.
Know Nature and know the Situation:
Triumph completely"
—Sun Tzu

What Is the Competitive Edge?

Good question. **The Competitive Edge** is about two things. The first one is obviously winning, because winning is important.

But how do we win? In both business and sports, winning with the competitive edge is about doing the things nobody else is doing. To have the edge, you have to be the best at what you do. You have to be better than everybody else.

That means working overtime to get the job done, right?

No, not always.

In search of the competitive edge, you must ask yourself a couple of questions:

- Is there a way I can do my job differently and wind up getting better results?
- What's not happening right now that needs to happen?

If you can look objectively at your production column and admit to yourself there is room for improvement, then the answer to the above questions is yes...absolutely. Nine times out of ten, there *is* an opportunity out there for you to take a better approach.

Most people would tell you that **working harder** than the competition is the *only* better approach—the *only* way to get a competitive edge. That's true—but only in a way. People who go the extra mile do often tend to be the people who win out in competition, whether that competition is professional or athletic. But sometimes working harder just isn't enough. Sometimes working harder isn't even *necessary.*

So this chapter isn't going to tell you that finding a competitive edge means working harder than the other guy. In this chapter you're going to learn something a little different.

Finding a competitive edge is a three-step process. The first step is identifying the tools in your own toolbox—in other words, what is it you do well already. The second step is identifying what the *competition* does well. And the third step is developing ways to sharpen your own competitive edge in order to bypass that same competition.

CLICK! Gaining a competitive edge starts with asking what's not happening—right now—that you need to happen.

The Many Faces of Competition

But before we can even get into any of these three steps, we first have to figure out *who* exactly your competition is. You'd be amazed at the number of people I have worked with who can't even properly list their competition let alone point out what it is they are doing to get an edge or steal clients away. So let's sum up this concept.

The competition—your competition—could be another individual in your daily life, the other team on the playing field, an associate at work, a law partner at your firm, or another company operating in the same market as your own. But these are all the clean-cut definitions of competition.

It gets deeper.

Competition can be something as **simple** as a corporate report nipping at your heels. It may be a golf course you like to play—or maybe just one particular hole on that course—that has always given you trouble. It could even be as **insignificant** as one specific shot on one particular hole (I usually have trouble with a downhill lie). It could be that thirteenth mile of a marathon or a challenging ski run. **Doesn't matter.** The point is that competition isn't always an entity. Competition is anything we must face that presents a particular challenge.

But you will notice the words I set in bold in the above paragraph: "simple," "insignificant," and "doesn't matter." Why did I do that? I did that because people tend to view these internal struggles—these obstacles to growing as an individual or gaining a competitive edge—as simple and insignificant. And I'll demonstrate in a second that internal resistances are just **the opposite.** Many times they are the *most* significant obstacles lying in our path and the *least* simple struggles to overcome.

More often than not, our biggest competition is ourselves. Sometimes that's easily identified, but oftentimes it's not.

The first step in identifying what's preventing you from gaining the competitive edge is to recognize that both inside and out of your own mind you are almost constantly competing. Recognize also that you're not the only member of this competition who is seeking an edge. Fortunately for you, there is only a very slim likelihood that the other competitors will follow the strategic *Click!* system. Instead, they will all continue to employ **conventional wisdom**. They'll all continue to attempt accelerating what they are already doing. They'll continue to work themselves harder and harder rather than take the time to **consider another approach**.

And there's your edge. While your competition is running like a hamster in a wheel, tripping over themselves and their personal, often unrecognized challenges, you will find the opportunity to adapt and take a different approach.

Doing the Small Things

When I talk to people about competitive edge, they're usually floored when I use the word "small" to describe it. Most of these get-ahead concepts are vast, sprawling, step-by-step methods designed to change an entire corporate or personal philosophy. But it's the small things that make the biggest difference in everything—competition, communication, corporate or personal strategy, you name it.

Take this example. One little word can change the entire scope of a competition. A few years back, my friend Don Gabor sent me a book he had written, *How to Start a Conversation and Make Friends*. When I finished, I wanted more of Don's material, so I picked up a copy of *Words That Win*. Somewhere along the line, the author of these two great books brought up the significance of the word "today" when used in the right context.

When is the last time you walked up to somebody you didn't know and asked, "How you doing?" You probably do it every day. We *all* do.

Now think about the response you get most often to that bland question that almost everyone asks a half-dozen times a day. What did you come up with? The responses I think of are things like "Good" or "Fine" or even "Great." Canned answers to a canned question. No way to start off a conversation with somebody you've never met. Exchanges like this usually end with an awkward silence. That's because neither participant in the conversation has given the other something to go on.

Now here's what I learned from Don's books, and I want you to try this for me. Next time you go out in public and you have the opportunity to ask this same question to a stranger, tack the word "today" onto the end of the question—as in, "How you doing today?" Just give it a try. You'll be *amazed* at what happens.

So What Happens?

The short answer is that the person you ask this question to is likely to launch into a long summary about how his or her current day is going. If you're talking to a cashier at the supermarket, you might hear about spills in aisle three, a slave-driving boss, and how it took an hour to get to work this morning because the city doesn't know how to plow snow. If you're talking to a stranger wearing a business suit in the hotel elevator, you may hear an oratory on an exhausting conference or company meeting; you might hear comments about a husband or wife; you might hear prideful stories about children.

The point is that one simple word, "today," for whatever

reason gets people to open up. It gets people *talking*. And in business as well as in life, talking is **exactly** what you want people to do.

Try implementing this one simple word into the management structure of your company. The next time you approach a colleague or employee about current projects, ask him or her how things are going *today*. The result in the workplace has given managers a tool to make their people feel more cared about. And it *really* opens up the lines of communication.

Little things like this get us ahead of our competition. It's finding out what can be done *differently*, what nobody else is doing, and then adopting it into our repertoire.

CLICK! One small change can make a huge difference in the outcome.

Obstacles to Your Competitive Edge

Now that we've had a taste of what competitive edge is, we can now move on to figuring out just how to exploit any potential edge you may find. Know this: the edge will likely be small, manageable, and (this is the best part) completely invisible to your competition. In other words, the **best competitive edge** is one that cannot be copied by competitors.

The best way to summarize this concept is by taking a more negative approach. In order to determine *how* to get your competitive edge, we have to address everything currently standing in your way. I've identified a nice round five obstacles to gaining a competitive edge. They are:

1. Distraction
2. Worry
3. Discomfort
4. Improper focus
5. Emotion

All these obstacles play **crucial roles** in everyday life, and many might be standing in your way, both professionally and personally, whether you realize it or not.

Obstacle #1: Distraction
Let's return to a golf analogy to highlight this point.

Imagine…for a moment…that you're on a golf course. You're getting ready to tee off on the first hole. You rifle through your bag for a ball and a tee. Head down, you walk into the tee box and set your tee at a comfortable height. You stand up, bend your knees, take a couple of practice swings, and then look ahead at the fairway for the first time.

You see the beautifully manicured grass, waving tree branches, a sand trap or two, maybe a water hazard. None of that bothers you, though. What bothers you are the piles of garbage; rusted out, wheelless cars; and discarded kitchen appliances littering the fairway. Your concern is with the crater-sized divots and imposing prairie grass beckoning from the rough. You worry about the garbage dumpsters lined up on the green—and wonder what on earth they are doing sitting next to mountains of corporate recyclables.

Of course, none of us has ever seen a golf course that looks like this, but if we had, the debris wouldn't have been any less distracting than the many things we tend to worry about each day. Even on a typically tranquil, completely peaceful golf course, many of us have a hard time overcoming our most fearsome competition—our own mind game. And that mind game can be **negative**. That mind game can be **distracting**.

Whether we're playing a legend named Tiger or an accountant named Stan, we focus on the wrong things. Things like what our competition has just done, our last shot, or numerous personal or professional issues that have entered our mind rather than what we must now do—even if the **only** concern we should have in the world is the three-iron shot we've got lying before us.

These are distractions. And distractions *are* competition.

Distractions can be costly. A salesman may not be able to close a sale because he's spending all his time on the phone thinking about how he just got rejected on the deal of a lifetime. A golfer may triple bogie the sixteenth because she's focused on the two-stroke lead she gave up way back on the ninth.

In addition to concentrating on failure, a person could compete within himself or herself over a particularly ineffective belief system or a traditional way of thinking about or approaching a given situation. All of these things add up to one thing: lack of focus. Without focus you will never win any kind of competition—not those on the playing field, and not those in the office.

Obstacle #2: Worry

Do you ever worry about things? Of course you do. You worry about getting the kids dressed, fed, and ready for school. You worry about the big upcoming project at work. You worry about a recent tiff with your spouse. As working professionals, it's in our DNA to worry.

The trouble with worry is that it is one of the most intense obstacles out there. It is a distraction in itself—one that prevents you from thinking about the only thing that matters: the present. Right now. Today. This moment.

How can you focus on the present, right now, today, this moment if you are worried about things that occurred in the past or might occur in the future? The answer is you can't.

What if you could determine a way to move the distraction of worry to another time? What if you could, say, *Click!* your fingers and tell yourself to worry from five to five-fifteen? You could say, "Worry about that at five o'clock... Don't worry about it now." Would that make a difference? Would you be able to focus more on the present, more on gaining that competitive edge?

Of course you would. And I have learned over the years that this technique works as well in the professional world as it does in sports performance. I demonstrated a way to move the distraction of worry in Chapter 3 (see the "Trunk Card" segment), but let me tell you, there *is* a catch to this strategy: if you tell yourself to worry at five o'clock, then when five comes around, you *had better show up* or your mind won't play the game.

Obstacle #3: Discomfort

Corporate America seems to have adopted this culture of sticking with conventional wisdom ("Don't be different"). Really, that mantra exists in almost all social spheres, but it's most prevalent in the corporate setting.

Because we are programmed to go with the crowd, do what everybody else is doing, and follow procedure to the letter, the idea of branching out and taking a different approach tends to create discomfort. Discomfort is another obstacle to focus and the competitive edge.

Make no mistake, none of what I am going to be covering in this book will feel comfortable at first. But you must embrace the discomfort if you want to get that edge.

I had a client who ran a sales team that drove almost all of its sales with cold calling. Like most companies of this sort, my client's company saw middling success in sales as long as it cast a wide-enough net. One particular prospective buyer had always plagued this client, however. He confessed to me two things: 1) this buyer would represent the biggest sale his company had ever seen, and 2) no matter how hard he tried, no matter how many salespeople he assigned to call in, he could not land the sale.

So I asked my client to describe this buyer to me in intricate detail. He explained that the buyer was actually a company he was certain would have wide use for his products. It had deep-enough pockets to make such a purchase, but my client's contacts there just didn't seem receptive to any of my client's attempts to sell them on the value of his products.

But there was one little detail that stuck out to me. My client explained that the prospective buyer operated out of a building only two blocks away. He had an army of salespeople calling from cubicles to a building just down the street and visible from his own office!

"Wait a minute," I said to him. "Why don't you just walk over to the buyer's building, request a sit-down, and see if you can hammer out an agreement that works for them?"

Looking at my client, I thought maybe I had accidentally

stepped on his toes. "That's not company protocol," he told me. "We cold call."

This may seem like a rather simplistic anecdote, but it cuts right to the heart of the problem with our need to follow the leader, to avoid going against the grain. My client refused to do anything that was not "by the book." And you know what? If he had taken my advice and walked over to his buyer—if he had taken the opportunity to do something *different*—he probably would have made that sale or at least have had a chance to meet with someone.

Obstacle #4: Improper Focus

So we now know that distractions can be an obstacle to learning your competitive edge because they get in the way of your focus. We also know that discomfort can sometimes lead to problems in adapting to new strategies. That leaves one of the biggest obstacles—and the one most often overlooked. Even if you can get yourself to focus more often, you have to make sure you are focusing on the **right things**.

If you are a business person, imagine…the greatest moment of your professional life. When was the time you made the greatest move you have ever made to ensure your company's success?

Let's say you just landed the biggest account in company history. How would your colleagues and coworkers react? They would congratulate you. You might wind up receiving a bonus or even a promotion based on the fact you were able to make your company so much money.

But how much attention would be paid to *how* you managed to land that account? In most corporate settings, everybody would be so wrapped up in the fact you had hauled the big fish into the boat that they would fail to concern themselves with *how* you reeled it in.

In all things business, the money is not the important part. The *method* of getting that money is the important part. Unfortunately, in many cases, that focus is off-line.

Imagine…your toolbox once again. Flip to the illustration on the back page of this book. **Take a look at the toolbox**. At this point in the book we have not offered many tools to place in it. So it might look empty to you. But it isn't empty. There are tools in there you may not realize you have.

What am I talking about?

Imagine…for a moment…that you are the CEO of a business you've built from the ground up. Over the years your company has climbed the ladder until it has reached its present state of overwhelming success. During that time many things had to break right, and you had to make a lot of timely and important decisions and adjustments. In addition to that, you had to possess and use a whole range of skills to keep your company afloat and headed in the right direction. You had to be one hell of a talented individual. Can you say that to yourself?

Now, today, it is time for you to pass your knowledge on to the next generation. Your daughter will be taking over the reins, and she has just asked you, "Dad, what do you think are the talents of yours that helped make this company what it is today?"

Do you have an answer for that specific question? Many people don't. Now think about what you actually do for a living. Think about what you do for a hobby. Think about all the things you do in which you excel. If somebody asked you what it is that makes you so good at that one job/hobby/

interest, could you answer? Could you identify the talents you possess or the *method* for demonstrating that talent?

What I'm getting at here is that oftentimes, when somebody asks you to hand him or her a tool in your toolbox, you discover you may not even recognize that there is a tool sitting in the box to begin with. I asked a client who had built an enormously successful division of a multinational company how he had made it happen. He paused, spread his arms out wide and said, "I was just being myself." "Great response," I replied, "unless it was important to you that I learn what you know so I can help your division grow."

The truth is that most of us know a lot more than we are aware we know—even if we use that knowledge each and every day. Unconscious competence is very valuable but almost always difficult to transfer to someone else. If you don't know what you know, how can you possibly use it to mentor others? And of course if you cannot properly mentor others, your own success is limited to what you yourself can personally do at any given time.

This fourth obstacle to gaining a competitive edge can be overcome with two specific methodologies. One is to perform a SWOT Analysis, and another is to shift your philosophy to something I have decided to call You, Inc. For those interested in these concepts right now, flip to Chapter 6: You, Inc., and Chapter 8: Preparing to Meet the Competition Versus Winging It for more in-depth analyses of the subjects.

Obstacle #5: Emotion

Earlier in this book I mentioned my client who is an ultramarathon runner. I have no trouble saying she's one of the best athletes in the world. Why am I so certain? One of her biggest events is a 135-mile run through Death Valley. First off... imagine running 135 miles. Now... imagine running it in 135-degree heat. I don't know how she does it.

The point is that doing what she does takes a great deal of focus. To help keep that focus, she has hired an entire support team to aid in her training and during her races. She has vans that trail her, people who monitor her heart rate and body temperature, and trainers who hand her icepacks, water, and even food. Essentially, she has a dedicated group of people who do everything they can to help her reach the finish line as quickly as possible.

Given the fact that we are talking about a race that's over a hundred miles, spanning several days, and taking place in heat so oppressive as to make one lose a grip on reality, mistakes are easy to make. Several years ago, during one such race, a couple of key members of her crew made some critical mistakes with monitoring her water and food intake. She grew exhausted faster from the overeating and drinking. But more important, the fact that her seasoned support team had made such a rookie error angered her. Actually, it *infuriated* her. So coupled with her exhausted body, she ran angry. Because of her anger she could not focus on her pacing, listen to her body, or manage her position in the pack. The race, obviously, was a disaster.

"I learned that day I can't afford to race angry," my client told me. "It's okay for me to be angry once the race is over, but never during."

My marathon running client makes a good point. Anger is okay. Venting is okay. But you have to *pick the right time* for it. When you are presenting to an audience, speaking to the media, performing an important task on or off the field, inside or out of the office, you cannot be angry. Anger will only weigh you down.

You can't make the call to your boss productive if you're angry about the actions of one of your employees. You won't reel in the next sale on your leads list if you're upset about letting the last sale slip through your fingers. You will not make a good putt if you are still furious about your drive into the woods.

Anger is only the most obvious emotion. The same goes for all the others, too. Emotions can get in the way of clear and levelheaded thinking. The key, then, to blocking out this common obstacle and maintaining your competitive edge is properly identifying your emotions and learning how to deflect them during competition.

CLICK! While there are many external obstacles, the internal ones are often more dangerous. What are yours?

The 8 Keys to a Competitive Edge

There are keys to **overcoming these obstacles** to **build a consistent, competitive edge**. As the title to this segment suggests, there are, in fact, eight. I mentioned them in the introduction and have taken some of them up as we went along, but since we are talking about the competitive edge, I'd like to lay them all out on the table for you right now.

As you review these strategies, be aware of a couple of

things. First, your competition is faced with many of the same challenges you are—and they often face them without an effective coping strategy. So the act of absorbing and adopting the strategies listed below is *itself* a competitive edge.

Second, the topics listed below are broad. Each key is discussed at length in some part of this book, and each represents one or more specific **tools** for your toolbox. Not all of them will apply to you now, but once you've read them and tried them and put them in the toolbox, they will be there when you need them. Feel free to pick and choose the ones you feel are most relevant to your given (and unique) situation. Do that, and in no time your toolbox will be full.

The 8 Keys to a Competitive Edge are:

1. Learn to control negative self-talk.
2. Identify your peak performance zone.
3. Prepare for competition.
4. Recover rapidly.
5. Employ power communication.
6. Adopt laser-strategic networking.
7. Influence and persuade with integrity.
8. Incorporate long- and short-range strategic planning.

In addition to offering these eight comprehensive strategies, this system is intended to provide many valuable extras. With your toolbox full, you will find yourself considering different approaches to business, sports, and life; implementing different ways of thinking; doing what others resist or will not do; training at persistence; turning knowledge into action; building speed, momentum, and consistency; controlling your mind game; breaking away from the crowd; and understanding how your competition traditionally operates.

CLICK! *It's a good idea to put tools in your toolbox as you find them.*

What Now?

Through it all, keep in mind that as you look at a particular challenge, some obstacles or roadblocks may be obvious. Only you can decide when or if you need more training, professional instruction, or better coaching. In business, you may find yourself thinking what you need is more product knowledge or sales training—but once you have finished with this book, you may discover what you really need is a **different application of personal or corporate strategy**.

Now that we have identified what a competitive edge is as well as some of the obstacles standing in the way of gaining that edge, we can resume identifying the tools that will help you achieve your goals. Read on to discover exactly how to put the *Click!* strategy into action.

Toolbox Tips

- Ask yourself what you can do differently—
  every day.
- Be aware of what is not happening—right
  now—that you need to happen.
- Know what your competition really is and
  name it.
- Notice all the obstacles that prevent you
  from getting your competitive edge.
- Put all 8 Keys to a Competitive Edge in
  your toolbox; you never know when you're
  going to need one of them.

CHAPTER 8

Preparing to Meet the Competition Versus Winging It

"Know the other, know yourself:
One Hundred challenges without danger;
Know not the other and yet know yourself:
One triumph for one defeat;
Know not the other and know not yourself:
Every challenge is certain peril.
Know Nature and know the Situation:
Triumph completely"
—Sun Tzu

Back to the *Art of War*. This whole book is clearly about preparation and execution. Look at the tools you've already dropped into your toolbox. You understand your **competitive edge**. You've read about the power of **imagining success**. You've learned how to become a **better communicator** (and there's plenty more of that in Chapter 10). You've got your **wish list** and a whole new understanding of You, Inc. And there are plenty more tools to come.

Right now… If you take a look at the highlighted passage in the quote above, you will see when it comes to **preparing for competition**, Sun Tzu really knew what he was talking about. Conventional wisdom dictates that when an important project, trial deposition, or football game is coming up, we must prepare. Preparation is critical. Otherwise, every challenge becomes certain peril.

But as you've seen and will continue to see again and again in this book, conventional wisdom too often falls short.

Winging It

On a radio program just the other day I was talking with the host about improving your golf game by working on your Mind Game Strategies. Here's what came up.

Q: Can you improve your golf game without practice?
A: Of course not.

Short game, long game, woods, irons, putting—all facets of the game of golf require plenty of practice and professional instruction. But then, so does anything you want to get better at—from playing the guitar to public speaking to selling widgets. There's conventional wisdom again falling short. Let me tell you, practice and professional instruction are not enough. There's more to it than that.

So the next obvious question has probably already come up in your mind: **What has conventional wisdom missed?** More important, **how does figuring out what's missing give you the edge?**

Preparing to Meet the Competition

Many NFL teams **plan** the first fifteen plays of a game. They **script** out their first offensive drive. These plays—among many others—are practiced over and over again as a team. The players are told to review them mentally even months before the season begins, the night before the game, and often seconds before the snap.

Strengths, Weaknesses, Opportunities, and Threats—a sports SWOT Analysis—flows from the minds of both offense and defense as they prepare to play and spend time in strategy meetings with coordinators prior to games.

For quarterbacks, the process becomes even more complicated. The mental screen must always be running, a process that results in almost continuous adjustments. They must attempt to see the whole field at once. They must visualize making no errors, committing no turnovers, and keeping possession of the ball, moving it downfield.

All of this preparation—this conventional preparation—in spite of the fact they will have a full four quarters and literally dozens of opportunities to run play after play in the attempt to drive to the goal line, score, and win the game. Each play requires tremendous effort and coordination.

But **imagine**...for a moment...a football game that involves only one play. How much more would those coaches, linemen, quarterbacks, and other position players practice and prepare if they had only **one play** to win the game?

And what if in our one-play scenario there was literally only one opportunity, one instant to succeed?

CLICK! *One "play" can make the difference*
between winning and losing—
even if you have many "plays" to get
your desired outcome.

Knowing the Competition

Imagine…for a moment…that the year is 1971 and you are NY Jets right guard Dave Herman. For many, this may be a difficult thing to imagine. In his prime, Dave Herman was a 270-pound professional offensive guard. And his primary task on a weekly basis was protecting one of the great quarterbacks of the era, Joe Namath.

Now, **imagine**…for a moment…that the ball has been spotted by the referee, and you, Dave Herman, line up beside it, several other 270-pound linemen to your left and to your right. You touch your fingers to the rough grass and listen for Namath's barking voice. You look up. Standing across from you, breathing like a man possessed, is Bubba Smith, one of the greatest defensive linemen of all time.

There you are…a 270-pound NFL lineman. And your job is to keep a six-foot-eight, 350-pound Bubba Smith from getting to the quarterback.

The ball is snapped…and in an instant you have effectively controlled the bigger man.

How was it that Dave Herman was able to do this? How could the smaller man prevail?

Conventional wisdom tells us that Dave needed to practice hard; Dave certainly practiced hard. Conventional wisdom tells us that Dave needed to know the game plan; Dave knew that offensive playbook inside and out. Conventional wisdom tells us that Dave needed to know his own limitations, what he could do and do it well; through rigorous training Dave had come to know himself and his abilities.

The problem with conventional wisdom is that it fails to take one thing into consideration: all week, Bubba Smith was doing the same thing.

So how does the physically overmatched Dave Herman get the edge? By taking conventional wisdom one step further: **You must know your competition in order to seize your instant of opportunity.**

For the offensive guard in the NFL, part of the preparation, part of knowing the competition, involves watching game films. So I asked Dave what he looked for when he reviewed these films in the week leading up to the game.

"I realized," Dave said, "that when a man that big begins to move forward, there's always an instant when he must be on one foot. So I waited until the foot came up, and that's when I took him down."

In many scenarios in today's business world, that's exactly what the professional must deal with. In business, you have only one shot at gaining the upper hand. You have only one shot at a touchdown.

CLICK! Everybody has access to the conventional wisdom and will behave accordingly; how can you take it just one step beyond the expected?

Mistakes

So knowing this, you need to be able to spot the mistakes—those moments when that giant defensive lineman is standing on only one foot—your own mistakes, the mistakes of the competition…and you must *learn from them.*

Learning from other people's mistakes can give you just the edge you need; it can even save you a fortune… Let's take a look at a couple from business situations.

An investment banking managing director I recently worked with lamented that two of his associates had blown a deal. He felt that because the associates had proven unprepared to deal with a difficult client, he had been wrong to trust them with the task.

"I should have done it myself," he reasoned.

So I asked him, "When did you role-play with them prior to the meeting?"

Silence.

"You mean you didn't take the time to give them a walk-through of the client meeting?" I asked. "You didn't assess their weaknesses before you let them proceed?"

You guessed it… This frustrated managing director hadn't taken the time to do the prep. Had he sat down with his associates and taken a look at the client's representatives and their principles and personalities, asked the right questions, and understood the individual goals and objectives of those involved before the presentation, the associates might have been in a better position to give the client's representatives what they wanted. Instead, they spent all their time trying to provide what *they thought* the client wanted. Sure, they were in command of the options at their disposal. They knew what they had to do. But there was a significant and critical piece missing: They didn't know with whom they were dealing. They didn't know *how* to sell that very specific client.

But a more hands-on traditional management style alone doesn't cut it. As an executive, you can't simply sit down and tell your employees what to do. That's like being the coach of the New York Jets, handing Dave Herman the playbook, and telling him all he will need in order to level Bubba Smith is to memorize the plays.

Something's missing here…

A senior partner at a successful law firm took exactly this kind of approach with a young lawyer in the firm. The lawyer had been assigned to one of the firm's most important cases of the year, so naturally she was a little nervous.

"So do you know what it is we want you to accomplish for the [XYZ] trial?" the senior partner asked the young lawyer.

"I'm not really sure," she said. "Why don't you give me some suggestions?"

Now… Here is where the senior partner made his mistake. Whereas the investment banking director didn't do enough to help his associates prepare their game plan, the senior partner did too much. He spent the next six hours with the lawyer, outlining *exactly* how *he* would approach the case and what to do in *any* situation he thought could arise.

"Here are the things we want you to accomplish," he said. Then he spent the better part of his day listing them. The young lawyer feverishly took notes and made diagrams. When the meeting was finished, she headed out to try to cobble everything together.

What he failed to remember is that he wasn't trying the case, she was. Her hand in the matter could produce any number of unforeseen outcomes. The case could have turned in an entirely different way than the senior partner had planned.

And then, all that careful planning might as well have been thrown out the window.

Fortunately, this senior partner and I were able to have a meeting before the young lawyer went to trial. When I presented him with the solutions I'll be covering in the next section, he was shocked by how much more he could have done—and in less time!

"What would you have lost if she would have gone to trial so unprepared?" I asked.

The senior partner looked almost ill. "There probably would have been a judgment of at least half a million dollars," he said. "And we would have definitely lost the client, one of our best—and that would have cost twenty million."

So in the fifteen minutes of implementing the strategy that follows, this law firm would have saved millions. The value of preparation—the *right kind* of preparation—is always worth a fortune.

---

*CLICK! When you need team members
to perform well, there's a critical
balance between giving them too little
and giving them too much. Either extreme
could cost the outcome you need—
and the money that goes with it.*

Coaching Culture:
Preparation for a Competitive Edge

In all but a few situations, simply having greater product knowledge does not necessarily translate into a competitive edge. When looking at top-performing companies, we must assume the highest level of product knowledge after all. The edge must come from something else. And it's often invisible.

When the edge is discovered, it usually involves the relationship with the client. At some point the client begins to feel you understood him or her. You project the notion that you understood the challenges and that you have a sense of the real dynamics going on in his or her world. But not every business relationship evolves to this point. Not all relationships are carried on forever, either.

So let's say *you* are the senior partner from the law firm we discussed a little earlier. You have reached into your toolbox, selected the proper tools for the job, and *really* prepared. The result is a winning strategy.

Now...imagine...for a moment...that you have gotten this strategy so deeply imbedded within yourself that it happens automatically. It has become the perfect representation of unconscious competence. The way you apply your trial strategy is akin to the wide receiver who does not have to think about running his routes; he just goes out and runs them.

Things have changed. Trials in which this unconscious strategy apply are no longer yours to handle. You have associates or partners to whom you must delegate the task. The firm may require you to assign newer lawyers (like the young lawyer from our earlier example) to trials you used to breeze through on your own.

On some level you must be feeling uncomfortable about

the idea. How can you know these young lawyers have properly prepared? Do they **know** how to win? Do they have the right **tools** for the job?

How do you know?

So imagine our same scenario from earlier. You are the senior partner. Only this time you are in a meeting with the young lawyer, and you listen as she discusses the case with a few of her colleagues. You expect to hear her strategy for the trial but what you hear are questions—what you interpret as a clear indication that she is *not* prepared.

Lucky you caught it in time. You think, *What if I hadn't dropped in on this conversation? What if I had allowed this young lawyer to go to trial thinking she was prepared when clearly she wasn't?*

You tell yourself she would have lost the case. *What do I do now?* you wonder.

Well, as we learned earlier, most people in a management position would have interrupted the conversation and explained to the lawyer *exactly how* to go about winning the trial. But hold on. Let's back up and see how a change in management strategy might have resulted in a more favorable outcome. There's got to be a better way. For her and for you.

There is...

If that senior partner and his firm had known to invest in building a **Coaching Culture**, the end result of the hours of preparation put in would have gone much more smoothly. And the outcome would have certainly been favorable.

Traditional management culture assigns a task, maybe drills the steps to completing that task into the heads of the employees, and then reviews the performance *after* completion. Sometimes this review occurs *months* after completion.

Why not complete the review *first*? Why not get it out of the way before the action even occurs?

Wouldn't that lead to better results?

But how do you do that?

Let's go back to the law firm. In the following scenario, the senior partner asks the *right* questions—questions designed to get the young lawyer to **take responsibility** for the trial on her own; questions that will help ensure that the **right strategies and steps** are being communicated; questions that will help the senior partner sleep better.

"So how do you plan to approach the [XYZ] trial?" you, the senior partner, ask the young lawyer.

"I'm not really sure," she says. "Why don't you give me some suggestions?"

You, the senior partner, probably have some ideas on how to approach the situation that the young lawyer has found herself in. But you *can't* tell her those ideas. Not yet anyway.

"Let's hear what you've got," you say. "Pretend I'm Mr. [XYZ]. Let's hear your strategy."

You must play the role of the client, Mr. [XYZ], and you must resist the temptation to jump in with your own ideas on how to proceed. You must not dictate. You must not critique. You must simply **ask** the right questions. And you must **listen** to the answers.

So what are the right questions? The three most important Coaching Culture questions the senior partner—or any person in a position of leadership—can ask an employee are:

1. What's your strategy for [this task]?
2. Is there anything you can think of that could get in the way of you getting the outcome you want?
3. What do you need from me?

Question 1 gathers any information the employee has already prepared for the task and helps the employer understand where the employee stands and whether he or she is headed in the right direction. Question 2 cuts more to the heart of the matter, however; it really forces the employee to dig deeper and actually discuss whether there are any obstacles in the way. Once he or she has brought the obstacles to light, he or she will be in better position to avoid them. We discussed obstacles at length in Chapter 4. It may be worth revisiting, because it's an important tool to consider as we move forward.

When it comes to Coaching Culture, however, question 3 is perhaps the most important question of the group—and for good reason. This question gets the team member—the young lawyer or whomever—thinking about what *the member* needs, not about what *you* expect of him or her. It gets the employee to take ownership of the problem and work *with* you rather than *for* you on coming up with a solution. Questions like this tend to ease the stress associated with delegating tasks and lead to fewer errors on the part of the employee.

What do I mean by that? Well, if you consistently asked your employees what they needed rather than telling them what you expected of them, you wouldn't have to worry as much about whether your employees were grasping everything you were telling them, would you? They would *tell you* what they know, rather than the other way around.

Employees working in this situation become more **independent**. They take a greater sense of **responsibility** for their assigned tasks. Even the tedious tasks start to seem less like chores and more like a part of the employee's development. And all of this will lead to better preparation on a more consistent basis. You'll find yourself spending only fifteen minutes per day asking the three Coaching Culture questions instead of three hours per day figuring out what went wrong.

Meanwhile, you're going to sleep better. Even when the most critical tasks for your company's success are coming up, you'll *know* your employees have done everything in their power to prepare properly simply because you've taken the time to learn what they are thinking and have had the opportunity to adjust that thinking as needed. You'll *know* whether you have the right people set up to complete the job. You'll *know* your employees have taken responsibility for the task and its deadlines. And you'll *know* exactly how that big meeting is going to go.

But the best part about this Coaching Culture strategy is that you need to ask these questions only two, maybe three times. Once you have established that you expect your employees to take the responsibility to be able to answer your three questions, they will do exactly that on a consistent basis. You will find that your employees come readily prepared to meetings with the answers to your three questions in mind before you even ask them. Better still, you will find that your employees will begin to *volunteer for tasks*—even the less interesting ones—simply because they will begin to view projects as part of their development rather than tedious jobs to complete.

So you see the **power** in all of this? It takes all the hand-holding out of the corporate environment. People quit waiting for their superiors to tell them what to do; they simply go out and do it. And a Coaching Culture makes delegating tasks that much easier too. It takes the responsibility of delegating off the shoulders of the employer and gets the employees volunteering for tasks.

CLICK! Worksheet 20:
My Coaching Culture can help you stay
on track with a coaching approach. You might
also want to engage individual or group
performance coaches on occasion.

It Never Stops

Coaching never ceases. Remember that NFL teams practice their plays over and over again, continuously. Similarly, you must make a commitment to asking the right questions of your employees, and you must make a commitment to preparing properly for the competition.

Implementing a Coaching Culture in your business will provide you with some obvious benefits:

1. You will become more comfortable with your staff's ability to process, plan, and prepare.
2. You will quickly spot errors in approach and strategy.
3. You will be better able to assess the abilities of your employees to respond to challenges.
4. You will be able to identify areas of development that should be focused on in future training.
5. You will save a tremendous amount of your time in helping your employees prepare.

6. You will know what your employees need from you in order to succeed.

Team members benefit from a Coaching Culture as well:

1. Your employees will become more empowered, self-reliant, and independent.
2. Your staff will spend more time researching, planning, and preparing prior to talking to senior leadership.
3. In the future, employees will understand that coming to a meeting with you means coming prepared with a strategy.
4. In the future, tasks that would have otherwise seemed tedious will feel more like a part of personal and professional development.

What Now?

Throughout this chapter I've repeated the phrase "asking the right questions." I have provided you with three critical questions to ask in any coaching situation. But there are obviously situations where more or even different questions apply. So how *do* you ask the right questions?

Well, you know you're asking the right questions when you feel you can:

- **Anticipate** objections before they happen.
- **Lead** your employees to address at least three or four things you don't want to have happen.

- **Guide** your employees to finding at least three or four solutions to those perceived problems before they come to you.

The best way to do this is to start approaching your employees, your tasks, your business, your competition, everything, from a very different direction. To truly anticipate and avoid obstacles, you and your employees must begin by working backward. You might want to go back to Chapter 5 and take a look at the 180 Degree Strategy. It's all about being prepared!

Toolbox Tips

- Remember that sometimes everything hinges on one chance.
- Prepare for every important event.
- Anticipate what the conventional wisdom will dictate—and get beyond it.
- Develop a coaching-based approach to management—even if you are managing only yourself.

CHAPTER 9

Why Stuck Is Not the Worst Place to Be

"Know the other, know yourself:
One Hundred challenges without danger;
Know not the other and yet know yourself:
One triumph for one defeat;
Know not the other and know not yourself:
Every challenge is certain peril.
Know Nature and know the Situation:
Triumph completely"
—Sun Tzu

Everyone knows how "stuck" feels:

- Sales are flat.
- Deals are not closing.
- Partners won't even talk about change.
- There's no sign of a promotion.
- You're not sure you're in the right field.
- You have opportunities but are not sure which one to take.
- You seem blocked when you try to manage down—or up.

- You can see the political landscape but aren't sure what to do next.
- Something just doesn't feel right.

Even reading that list is kind of overwhelming. You feel it, the company feels it—we all feel it. We're doing what we have always done—what's worked before—and maybe we're doing more of it. In spite of this, not much—or not enough— is happening. Deals are getting almost there but simply not closing; responses are slow to come or stopping altogether; and the conversations you know you need to have are not happening.

Confronted with this, most of us get very antsy. We struggle to end up anywhere but here, stuck in neutral with that uncomfortable sense of being overwhelmed.

But consider this… It could be worse.

You could be moving rapidly in the wrong direction, making the wrong moves, saying the wrong things at the wrong time to the wrong people. You may have heard the statement, "When you realize you're in a hole, the first thing to do is to stop digging." That's easy to say from the outside. When you're on the inside, you can be aware there are obstacles, but they can be invisible at the time.

A very successful business guy asked me to help him with a very important piece of his golf game. It didn't involve his equipment, his swing, or instruction; his teaching pro would take care of that. Instead, he needed help with an invisible obstacle. Something was happening consistently that he couldn't figure out. He told me, "I've developed a hitch in my swing. At the top of my backswing I do this weird lift. My friends notice it." I asked him to describe to me when it happens.

You may be surprised to discover it happened only when

his ball was sitting perfectly in the fairway, never when it was in the sand or in a difficult lie. As successful as he was, I asked if he had ever been in a situation with his business where he was about to "blow it wide open" and somehow he put a "hitch" in the deal. He thought for a while—so I asked him whether it sounded possible, even if he couldn't name the specific circumstances. He said yes. As he reflected on these key deals and described these key situations, it became clear that he recognized a pattern.

But when I asked if he wanted to explore it, he said no and left.

To get the edge you have to want it, see where you want to be, identify obstacles, and move with momentum and consistency. You have to grab it.

It's About a Lot More Than "Right Now"

Not everyone looks the other way or sits and stews when he or she is stuck. When the CFO of a communications company felt that her firm was stuck, she got me in front of the three principals. From other sections of this book you've probably figured out that my initial approach was to figure out what they actually *wanted* to happen. So I had them go through the Magic Wand of 20XX, asked each principal what his life would look like, what the company would look like, and so on.

The 20XX five-year-out strategy can involve a few hours for an individual and longer for a team, but the results can be incredibly revealing. In this case the first principal said he wanted to triple the company's annual revenue from $10 million to $30 million. The second—much to the surprise of the other two—said he wanted to cash out during that five-year period. And the third wanted a partial exit that would allow him to continue working with the firm under a consulting arrangement. No wonder the CFO thought they were stuck; you can put a car in only one gear at a time!

Clearly, each leader had a different idea of where he wanted to be and sent that message unconsciously. Because of the fragmented management styles, marketing, sales, and admin were largely directionless—a management nightmare. In this situation each partner was stuck. I worked with them to complete a process of redesigning their company towards their individual goals and objectives. This was a much easier task once the obstacles were identified.

Another client—the president of the US division of a global company based in Australia—said his sales had stalled. At our initial breakfast meeting I asked, "What do you want to happen in five years?" "Triple the size of the company," he replied. He then described a few situations nationally with his sales team and really gave me the 1,000-foot view of the company. Things looked quite interesting until I found out he had twenty-two people reporting to him. I told him I enjoyed the meeting but wasn't sure I could help.

He was surprised to say the least. But I pointed out he would be even worse shape if he tripled the size of the company and had sixty-six people reporting to him. He was essentially stuck because his own management style handcuffed him. I reminded him that Carly Fiorina, former CEO of Hewlett-Packard, would limit direct reports to seven people. It took us about four months, but the restructure put him on a far more positive track. The process—and his desire to get the edge— uncuffed him and his leadership team.

Getting unstuck can work—and present a great opportunity

to figure out where you actually want to be instead. Knowing you're stuck is where it starts.

What Now?

"We're stuck!" means different things to different people in different situations. It can involve interpersonal relationships in business (especially in family business) and private life, it can involve performance in business and sports, and it can involve focus issues. The important thing is to notice when you're stuck and identify it as an opportunity to move forward with greater strategic purpose. Being stuck is really little more than your subconscious telling the rest of you that things are out of alignment—and you need to bring them back. The tools in this book will help you do exactly that.

CLICK! Use Worksheet 22:
My Sense of "Stuckness" to help you
identify why exactly you are stuck.
You can then use Worksheet 9: My Magic
Wand of 20XX to rechart your course.

Toolbox Tips

- Remember that going in the wrong direction is far worse than being stuck.

- Keep in mind that stuck is not as much about where you are as about where you want to go.
- Determine the underlying conflict or concern holding you back.
- Move beyond it by envisioning where you really want to be.

CHAPTER 10

Communication Strategies for Peak Performance

*"**Know the other, know yourself**:*
One Hundred challenges without danger;
Know not the other and yet know yourself:
One triumph for one defeat;
Know not the other and know not yourself:
Every challenge is certain peril.
Know Nature and know the Situation:
Triumph completely"
—Sun Tzu

Positive and confident communicators are not born. They are made.

I kick off this chapter with that statement for good reason. We've all met men and women who seem to be natural speakers. They manage to woo crowds. They're great at parties. They can talk their way out of (or into) anything they want. These people are known as **Power Communicators**. I've met my fair share of such communicators, and I can tell you firsthand that some of them may be born with the propensity to speak but none had obtained that compelling skill without hard work.

But to prove the point about how power communicators

are **not born** but **made**, let's take a look at the tremendous shift in culture among companies in this country. In this arena, the myth that you have to be a born communicator is being proven wrong every day. Companies now regularly invest in new tools and strategies to better serve their clients and to keep a competitive edge...and it's *working*. There was a time when companies questioned the cost of investing in communication training; today they are asking what it will cost them if they do *not* invest in this training.

Fortunately, practice for this sort of thing comes naturally, as we tend to communicate constantly, inside and outside the workplace. Power communicators understand, however, that not all communication is verbal. They *strive* to enhance all the aspects of their personal communication, including nonverbal signals. In fact, the nonverbal side of communication may very well be the most important piece of the puzzle.

In this chapter we'll explore the **foundations of communication**, highlighting the many aspects of verbal and nonverbal interaction that a power communicator must take into consideration in order to deliver a message effectively. We will also turn the lens inward and discuss the benefits of examining the way we speak to ourselves in order to gain a better understanding of how to speak to others. Finally, we will explore two keys to the mastery of power communication as well as a few methods for obtaining those keys.

But in keeping with this book's established structure, let's first address the most common obstacles before moving on to explain the methodology.

Common Personal Obstacles

As with anything, there are plenty of obstacles in the way of our becoming power communicators. If there weren't, everyone would be an effective speaker and listener (and the world would probably be a much better place). There are many common personal obstacles, but only a couple bear covering in detail in this chapter. Volumes have already been written in the hopes of eliminating the others.

The most common personal obstacles to success include:

- Negative self-talk
- Lower self-esteem and self-confidence
- Ineffective preparation (or winging it)
- Fear of success or failure
- Fear of embarrassment
- Procrastination
- Lack of awareness (of the person or people one is speaking to)

Internal obstacles are not easy to discover, but they can be destructive just the same.

A top saleswoman was having difficulty dealing with a specific client. No matter how much rapport she built with this client, she just didn't feel comfortable in her presence. As a result, she consistently found difficulty in closing sales. Since these were not insignificant sales, her inability to close carried a great impact on the company's bottom line.

But if the verbal communication was so great between the two, what was getting in the way?

In working together, this saleswoman and I discovered that the problem lay not in what was being said but in what was being *worn*. In short, the client frequently wore very expensive clothing. Something as simple as the clothing worn into the meeting room turned out to be the intimidating factor. We determined that this saleswoman's future success required that she identify and deal with her discovery, so she acquired some new wardrobe items she wore only when she met with that particular client.

The Foundations of Communication

"It's impossible not to communicate."

I've made this statement a few times during seminars, and it's almost always greeted with the same skeptical stares. The common reaction is, "That's ridiculous. I'm sitting here in this chair with my mouth shut. I'm not communicating right now... Am I?"

Yes... You *are*.

Don't fall into the trap of believing when you say nothing you are not communicating. Even if you're sitting in your chair quietly, let's not forget about that skeptical stare I mentioned. That stare tells me plenty, doesn't it?

Yes... It *does*.

Caution: Do you want to communicate the way you feel? Watch what message you send with body language. Somebody *might want to read it*.

Would you be surprised to discover that only six percent of communication occurs because of the words we use? It's true. It's remarkable how often people underestimate the value of what we call the subtleties of speech. In reality, these subtleties account for far more than we give them credit for.

In a moment I'm going to ask you to put down this book and start a conversation. It doesn't matter with whom; it can be a friend, a neighbor, a loved one, a coworker, an employer... anyone. When you have this conversation, you're going to want to pay attention to the words you and your speaking partner are using, but more than that, I want you to focus on the significance of the following points:

- **Voice tone...** Notice the tone and inflection of your voice. Is it different depending on whom you're speaking with?
- **Body language...** Listen to your body language. Hear the body language of others. What is your speaking partner doing with his or her hands? Posture? Facial expression? Now what are you doing?
- **Speech patterns...** Note the nuances of your speech. How fast are you talking? What key phrases are you using? How do they differ from person to person?
- **Eye contact...** Keep your eyes focused. How long do you hold eye contact? How steady is it? Does your partner meet your gaze or break away from it?

Take note of the items above. Mark them down in your mental notebook. Now put this book down and go start a conversation. When you return, write down your findings.

CLICK! Use Worksheet 23:
*My Nonverbal Communication Habits to
notice what messages you might be sending
to a variety of people.*

All these things speak volumes about our feelings for the person with whom we are talking, the topic in question, and the desire we have about being a part of the conversation in the first place, but none is more important than body language. People who study, observe, interpret, and act on the information they receive from body language rarely talk about it. Whether employed in a boardroom or a social interaction, these people (correctly) consider their information to be a competitive edge.

I was recently approached by a school board member who needed assistance with her on-screen presence. She had just finished reviewing the manner in which she conducted herself in a televised session. What she saw did not please her; she was exhibiting facial expressions, body movements, and hand and arm gestures that were sending messages she did not want to send.

Once I was at meeting in Geneva with an international businessman. I watched my client as he pushed his chair back from the table, leaned back in his chair, and put his hands behind his head while other people were speaking. Although he didn't realize it, he was clearly communicating his displeasure, distrust, frustration, and disagreement with other people at the meeting. The interesting part is that the client, while sending these less-than-desirable physical messages, remained totally unaware of the message he was sending—let alone that others might be able to read it. When I mentioned to him afterwards, he asked me how I knew how he felt. I told him that hopefully I was the only one in the room who could read how clearly he was sending a message.

. The key observation here is that each of these people had difficulty getting the message received by their audience to match the message they intended to broadcast. They had obviously prepared the content of their presentations in an effort to control the outcome, but that outcome just wasn't coming.

Make no mistake—this doesn't mean the words we choose are not important (we'll learn a little more about that later. Also, see Don Gabor's *Words That Win*), it just means that we must study and master *all* aspects of communication if we hope to become power communicators.

CLICK! Once you've become practiced
at observing yourself, try to actively observe
other people. Again, Worksheet 23:
My Nonverbal Communication
Habits might be helpful.

"It is important that we become aware of how we communicate with ourselves."

Over and over I hear the above statement from athletes, coaches, and CEOs. But since the focus here needs to remain on what works and what doesn't, let's take a brief look at this issue.

What I call the **Negativity Tape** is one of the three modes of self-talk. The other two are the **Positive Tape** and the **Corrective Tape**. These latter two tapes are those we will want to pay attention to moving forward—and we will learn how to identify and use them later—but for now let's get to an understanding of that first tape; it is likely to be the one that will lead to difficulty down the road.

The Negativity Tape is a kind of internal recording that lets us know exactly how and when we are screwing things up. It continues to remind us of our failures, sometimes over and over and over. As we will find out later, for some it is like a looping reel that plays over and over unless it is stopped. The reasons why it is so difficult to get out of a loop of negativity are threefold:

1. It takes some concentration to notice it.
2. People rarely discuss it—and so assistance might be close by but never called upon.
3. They may not realize they can control it.

The good news is that once identified, the Negativity Tape is easy to control—or at least shut down. As we move through these steps and strategies, be sure to remember you're not the only one with a tape to overcome. Remember, when your tape is running, *so is the competitions'.* And they aren't likely to be talking about it either.

You will notice above I asked you to note the ways in which your partner spoke, moved, and made eye contact… But also recall I asked you to write down how you behaved during the conversation.

How do you speak to yourself? As with anything else, negative self-talk tends to be a *huge factor* on your performance before, during, and after a speech, conversation, business deal, trial, or negotiation. It has the overwhelming potential to contaminate your performance and get you results you don't want.

I won't get too deep into this topic since this book includes a chapter on self-talk. (In fact, if this topic interests you, flip straight to Chapter 2), but the challenge is *first* to notice it is there.

Why is this so important? You can't control what you can't see, hear, or feel!

As you read this paragraph, listen and notice the way you are speaking to yourself within your mind. Identify **what is being said**...**when the talking starts**...**what environment it is connected with**...and **when it stops**. There are comprehensive methods to eliminating negative self-talk in Chapter 2, but it certainly bears mentioning here again as it has the potential to undermine any effort towards becoming a power communicator.

Observe that I have requested that you *listen* to your self-talk in order to determine its value or detriment to your communicative behavior. Listen. It is a substantial word. And it may seem cliché, but it has as much to do with communicating as does speaking.

Actually, it is the first of our two major keys to power communication:

Major Key #1: Effective Listening

Have you ever heard of somebody being described as a great listener? What was the expression on the face of the person describing this great listener? It was a pleasant expression, wasn't it? I've never heard of somebody described in this way in a negative light. That is simply because the average person appreciates a deep listener every bit as much as (if not more than) a "smooth talker." The Power Communicator, therefore, knows how to listen whenever it is warranted.

Since it is such a major key to communication, let's dub it **Power Listening**.

I remember a time when I was much younger and eating in a diner with my father. We did that sort of thing a lot when I was growing up, and I think I owe a great deal about my understanding of communication to those occasions. This particular day is applicable here. Dad and I were eating burgers in our usual corner booth when the door to the diner swung open. In walked a man wearing jeans and a leather jacket. It wasn't his tough-guy clothes that caught my attention, though. It was his black eye.

"Dad, look at that guy's eye," I remember saying.

"Yeah," Dad said, looking up briefly from his meal. "You want to know how that happened?"

I nodded excitedly, thinking maybe my dad had knowledge of the fight this man had obviously been in.

"Son, he got it because he was talking when he should have been listening."

For those who don't like the image of catching a black eye for talking out of turn, Dorothy Leeds, author of *Smart Questions,* quantifies the importance of listening with a much less violent story. She calls it "Staying Out of the Rain."

Imagine…that you are caught in a driving rainstorm.

You and a client are stuck under an awning, waiting out the deluge.

Now **imagine**…that as long as you can hear your client's voice you will remain dry. Whenever you hear your own voice, you find yourself standing in the rain once again.

Keep that in mind the next time you're speaking about an important topic with a client, friend, teammate, or family member. With any tenuous subject, listening is almost always what keeps you dry.

Effective Listening Strategy

Ever seen the movie *Heat*? Well, if you haven't, you should—particularly if you have any interest in examining the skills of listening. For one thing, the cast is spectacular. I suggest you rent the film.

As Antonio Saillant, writer, actor, and president of Angel Light Pictures once told me—strictly as a fan of great movies—the reason he likes *Heat* is based on one key scene. The scene in question features camera shots that focus on the actor who is *listening* instead of the one who is *talking*. It's illuminating to see how actors like Al Pacino and Robert De Niro react in such non-traditional filming. Both are clearly good listeners—if not simply great actors.

So how do we improve our listening skills? First, ask yourself the following:

- How well do I listen?
- Can I identify my barriers to listening?
- How much do I need accurate information?
- Can I learn more about my client's objectives with effective probing?
- What can I do to get better at active listening?

So given the importance of listening, the fastest path to becoming a Power Communicator is to learn how to listen effectively, right? Wrong! It is actually more important to start by recognizing when you are not listening.

One way this is carried out—and it's a strategy used often by athletes—is to identify distraction and, as they put it, identify it *quickly*. The second they are off-focus is the second they make a misplay. Not listening is one of the surest signs you are distracted—and there's no power in that for communication or anything else. Chapter 3 explores distractions in depth.

It Is the Responsibility of the Communicator That the Message Be Received

When people are attempting to convey things to each other, who's responsible for making sure the message is received and acted upon? We've talked about the importance of listening in communication, so it might seem it is the responsibility of the listener to **understand**, **interpret**, and **internalize** material and data spoken or presented by others. Indeed, this has often been the way we have viewed the exchange—and our parents start drumming it into us early on. Whether the venue happens to be a classroom, the kitchen table, the locker room, or the boardroom, the expectation is often the same:

If you don't listen and understand...the responsibility falls on you... It's your responsibility to understand... If you don't...you lose out.

This ought to sound very familiar to you even if you don't agree with it.

Well, I have both good news and bad news for you. This age-old lesson doesn't apply so much anymore. These days, more and more people understand that the listener's attention is at least as valuable as the speaker's intention. For every listener the speaker loses, that's one more situation spoiled, relationship lost, or business prospect that walks away disengaged. So it's up to the *speaker* to deliver the message in a clear, concise, and compelling manner. The *communicator* must understand who the listeners are and structure the message based on that knowledge.

Speech is free. We can say anything we want, any time we

want, in any way we want, and to anyone we want...just so long as we are not concerned about the outcome.

My father always said, "If you have something to say, think about the outcome you want. If what you're planning to say will get you your result, say it. If not, don't."

Since we are focusing on the **importance of outcomes**, we must consider the idea that it is our responsibility as aspiring power communicators to deliver a message that will be understood. This is simply because being misunderstood has grave consequences: it leads to a shortfall of the desired influence carried by the message.

Major Key #2: Effective Preparation

Recall the third of our most common obstacles to success in communication. Whether we are talking about presenting to a large group or carrying on a regular conversation, far too many people wing it. In the workplace, a power communicator—if the outcome is important—must consider a variety of factors as he or she prepares a face-to-face conference, staff meeting, community seminar, sales meeting, or employee review.

"Winging it," a term that describes a performance that relies solely on a person's experience, is a dynamic with a significant potential downside. Most high performers have become unconsciously competent; they perform very well without much forethought. This sort of thing works very well until the bar is raised. Sometimes it's easy to see the bar going up, but more often than not the change is imperceptible. You may not find out until it's too late that things were not as they seemed. This is why *strategy* becomes critical.

Get There Early

I once spoke to a small group who give those big corporate presentations as a career. Their *job* was to give speeches. I honestly thought effective preparation would be second nature to them. So I asked them a couple of questions—and was usually surprised at the responses. After your next presentation, ask yourself these same questions:

- At what point during your presentation did you feel you had built a bond with the audience?
- What if you had gotten there a half-hour before the presentation? Would that have made a difference?
- In almost every case the answer to the second question is yes. Getting there early and getting a feel for the setting of the presentation and those who will attend make all the difference in the world. Getting there early allows for time to ask your attendees questions about what they are looking for in your talk. Getting there early allows you to build a better bond with as many as five or six people in your audience. Getting there early allows you to determine exactly what information will be important to provide to the people in attendance.

Far too many people in the workplace simply stroll into a sales presentation or boardroom and present off the top of their heads. Consider for a moment how ridiculous that is. Knowledge of the person receiving the information is every bit as important as knowledge of the information itself. I mean, it is the same with every conversation, every speech, every presentation.

Sharpen Your Message

A professional speaker (some say it was Churchill) was asked how much time he needed in order to prepare a talk. He replied, "If you want me to speak for three hours, I can do it right now...no preparation. But if you want me to speak for one hour, it will take me a week to prepare. A fifteen-minute talk may take two weeks to prepare."

Whether the message is carefully designed and combed for content and presented or whether it is a messy and incomprehensible jumble of data, it can be improved.

Frequently (and unfortunately), the emphasis on most presentations these days is placed on product knowledge rather than knowledge of the recipient.

Let's shed some light on how knowing the person you're interacting with is the most critical aspect of every communication or relationship. Think about the last time you wanted a promotion. Everybody hits that stage at some point. Some people even live in it constantly. Now consider this phrase: "Do everything right, do a great job, and you will be noticed and promoted."

This is the short version, of course, but how true is it? I like to imagine the majority of my readers shaking their heads when reading that sentence. Far too often, people who have done all the right things are passed over for those better jobs.

I had a client who managed to upend this organizational tendency. "Jack" was on the director level of a large corporation. His next promotion—the one that just wouldn't seem to come—was to vice president of his department. A casual inquiry to HR revealed to Jack that he was still at least three years away from that coveted promotion—*if* everything went his way. The truly harrowing thing, though, is that he also learned that the higher-ups deemed him to be operating on about an even keel with no fewer than ten other directors.

This bothered Jack because he was in such a mission-critical division. Like the other ten directors, he maintained a high profile within the company, but unlike the others, it was also his responsibility to stand up to the external forces (the media, state and federal agencies, etc.). And he did it exceptionally well.

So there was Jack, doing a great job.

Now let's shift focus to Jack's superiors. To them, the status quo was nice and cozy. As far as they were concerned, Jack could and would continue to do what he was doing and continue to do it well. They didn't think they needed to promote him with any haste. Besides, if they did take such an action, they'd be left explaining to the other directors, who would ask, "Why him and not me?" No amount of explanation to a question like that would prevent the whole system from being thrown off balance. On the surface they had plenty of motivation to simply let all this ride.

Jack asked me to assist him with a strategy. Here it is: We knew his situation. We took a 1,000- foot view of his current standing and studied the personalities of the company's decision makers. As a result he discovered a dynamic that actually *strengthened* his position.

Jack went to the company board and informed them that, in his environment outside the walls of the company, he found that clients and prospects tended to prefer to deal with vice presidents (or comparable executives). Anyone calling in to speak to the department head wasn't going to be satisfied by being transferred to a mere director in that department. They wanted to talk to the VP—someone with clear authority to make a commitment or resolve an issue. This was especially true when the caller was on the same level at his or her company. A VP usually doesn't want to talk to a person in a position lower than his or her own.

Jack had a simple solution to this problem: assign leadership of each mission-critical division to a VP. Not only would that alleviate the disconnect when people were calling in, it would also be a clear sign that the company's leadership was serious about each division's initiatives—and its profile would certainly seem elevated.

So Jack took the purely personal out of the picture. He got those board members thinking not about what Jack wanted but about what *they* wanted. He also made it quite clear they weren't the only ones who would want such a promotion. In fact, their clients, other agencies, and the media would all welcome him warmly if he were a vice president.

Leadership, having seen the light, promoted Jack immediately. They simply felt *they* needed him as VP and the cost of not having him at that level was too great to bear.

Mental Preparation for Better Communication

As mentioned earlier, somewhere between an individual's skill, talent, preparation, and experience and his or her exceptional personal and professional performance, obstacles often get in the way. So in order to become better communicators, we must develop tools to anticipate, avoid, eliminate, or cope with obstacles.

I've said before in this chapter that you can't control what you can't see, hear, or feel. Understanding how different situations affect you (prior to entering a particular situation) places you in the position to adjust your behavior and allow for a better outcome. And so the first step in becoming better communicators is to use the detailed self-assessment that my clients use: the SWOT Analysis.

If you took the time to work through Chapter 5, you will already be familiar with the SWOT Analysis, but let me provide some additional context here. People typically employ this technique to evaluate their businesses, but it is every bit as valuable in summarizing their own communicative strengths and areas they may want to work on.

Strengths

First, list your strengths, or what you do well when communicating with others. This requires you to compliment yourself, which goes against much of what we were told growing up (you know, "Don't brag," etc.). But we must ignore these past influences because knowing what you do well will become important as you develop your team.

Understand that most high-performing people I work with find this difficult. Remember that you can't teach something you don't know you do. It is important in your strategy to apply these concepts to those with whom you will be dealing. Also, *always* begin with someone's strengths, particularly those you recognize and those they don't.

Weaknesses

Next, list your weaknesses, areas in which you could improve. I don't care for the word "weakness" because it's too negative, even abrasive. But it's the "W" in "SWOT Analysis," so we'll use it. Think about it as areas for improvement (although SAOT just wouldn't sound right).

To find your weaknesses—particularly if you're the kind of person too proud to mark down weaknesses in your mental notebook—I suggest you consider past interactions and performances that didn't work out for you. Recall how you inadvertently generated outcomes you really did not want. Within these memories you may find a list of things you would like to change.

Opportunities
Then list your opportunities. As you analyze your opportunities, think, **W-W-W-H**:

- **What** opportunities exist?
- **When** do they exist?
- **Where** do they exist?
- **How** do I take advantage of them?

Then apply the following by answering the questions for each situation:

Past Opportunities...no chance of recovery:
- What is your estimated cost of lost revenue?
- What could have happened that would have prevented this opportunity from passing you by?
- What did not happen?
- What communication issues got in the way of your meeting this opportunity?

Past Opportunities…recovery is possible:
- What can you learn from this missed opportunity?
- What would be the cost to you and/or your company if you do not recover from this missed opportunity?
- What three communication strategies might you use in order to recover?

Current Opportunities…the here and now:
- What opportunities are sitting in front of you right now?
- What kind of revenue do they represent for you and/or your company?
- What three communication strategies might you use in order to take advantage of them now?

Future Opportunities…the possibilities to come:
- What opportunities do you envision presenting themselves to you in the future?
- What kind of revenue do they represent for you and/or your company?
- What three communication strategies might you use in order to take advantage of them when they arrive?

Threats
The final portion of our SWOT Analysis calls for you to consider the threats to the achievement of your communication

goals. What are the **risks** or **costs** of leaving things as they are and doing nothing? Will personal relationships unravel? Will business be lost?

After you've done all this work, the next step to becoming a power communicator is a simple one. Before entering into a personal or professional conversation, we must ask ourselves one question:

Why am I communicating at this time?

This question is *critical* because determining the purpose of your communication will dictate your strategy when carrying it out. While the overarching question is quick and easy to remember, the questions leading up to a full understanding of the answer are a bit more complex.

In order to get to the bottom of why you are communicating on a particular occasion, you must first determine your goal in carrying out that communication.

Try the following exercise before your next significant communication, whether business or personal.

Ask yourself: What is my goal? Is it one [or a combination] of the following outcomes?

- To Inform: Do I just want to convey basic information?
- To Persuade and Influence: Do I wish to convince or encourage a specific behavior?
- To Educate: Do I aim to provide information so a decision can be made or teach my team?
- To Network: Do I need a concise and well-planned message, quickly delivered?
- To Motivate: Do I intend to inspire and encourage?

- To Coach: Do I plan to spur others on to higher levels?
- To Gain Information: Do I have more questions than answers?

Once you have answered these questions, you will find yourself with a proper foundation to work from in order to prepare effectively for the personal conversation, presentation, or professional interaction. The mental approach, however, is only one side of the coin; several obstacles to clean communication that occur on the physical side still remain.

Physical Preparation for Better Communication

I am five foot ten. At a recent event I was asked by a gentleman seeking a high-level PR position if I had any tips for him. He was about six foot two, which is fine, except that when he spoke to me, he stepped right into my space so I had to crane my neck to look at him.

"Well," I said, "to begin with, you should back up about two feet... You are way too close to me."

As he backed away, I found myself speaking and interacting with him more comfortably—which freed me up to think more effectively about the help he requested.

I had client who was a six-foot-seven, 277-pound prizefighter. When fighting, he needed to use his size to his advantage, but when he was talking, it put him at a disadvantage. He learned to position himself at eye level when he wanted to communicate with people.

It's funny to consider something so simple can make such a huge difference. But it really does.

Quick Tips to Improve Body Language:

1. If you are tall, try to position yourself at eye level with the person you are speaking to.
2. Never stand to negotiate. Always (politely) ask the other person to sit.
3. Do not get too close to an individual. Invading someone's personal space has the tendency to make that person uncomfortable, and discomfort always distracts from the message.
4. Make sure to keep your gestures close to your body.
5. Dress for success. (Trust me… Business casual is on the way out. It's always easy to remove your jacket or loosen your tie if the situation calls for it, but it is risky to arrive dressed down.)

Pacing and Leading

Have you ever had a conversation with a person who spoke so quickly and with such enthusiasm that you found yourself exhausted by the time he or she was finished? I know I've been in that situation many times. Have you ever been bored silly by a boss, presenter, pastor, teacher, or anyone else who spoke in a monotone? Who hasn't?

It is no secret that people like to deal with people like themselves—both on a personal and professional level. The more similar two people are, the greater their rapport. So when meeting someone new—particularly a prospective client or customer—if you can get your own speech patterns to match the pace and tone of his or her voice, you can expect to build rapport very quickly.

And body language plays in as well. If you notice the person you are speaking to nods his or her head a lot, you should nod your head as well. The other person will unconsciously begin to feel like he or she is talking to himself or herself.

One major key to success on the communicative level is mastery of pacing and leading. The trick is to bring your speech pattern in alignment with the person with whom you are speaking. When attempting to form this match, you must consider:

1. **Voice:** Consider several things about your voice to match it with your speaking partner(s) more quickly. You may even discover that you adjust to these things already without realizing it.
   - Speed of delivery: Notice how quickly or slowly people speak.
   - Volume: Are they loud or soft spoken?
   - Tone: What feelings or emotions are they projecting?
   - Vocabulary: Is their vocabulary vast or basic?
2. **Eyes:** People fix or move their eyes in many different ways. Incompatible eye movement can be a huge discomfort for some people.
3. **Head nod:** Some people nod their heads as they speak. Notice when it happens.
4. **Handshake:** Matching the handshake of

the other person is absolutely critical to effective communication. It sets the stage for the rapport building (or lack thereof) to come.

5. **Gestures:** Notice how a person gestures when speaking or making a point.

6. **Breathing:** Notice a person's breathing pattern. Studies have shown that people are most comfortable when they are with others who breathe at a pace similar to their own.

So what do you do with all this information? Well, as I have hinted, the closer you match the other person without mimicking too overtly, the more comfortable and at ease that person will be. Much of this happens subconsciously, but it is often effective in terms of building a positive communication.

Finally, before wrapping up the chapter, let's take a brief look at the concept of word choice.

The Power of Words

To put it bluntly, some words work, and others don't. And what better samples to draw from than the ever-increasing pool of trade jargon? Regardless of the business or industry, people develop jargon specific to that business. I provide the following list in order for you to reflect upon the power of words. On the left are commonly used terms in almost any industry. On the right are alternative words that tend to exact a more positive response from the listener.

Contract.................... Paperwork
Buy............................. Own
Cost .... Investment
Payments .... Installments
Sign............................ Okay
Signature................... Autograph
Approval .... Acceptance
Salesperson................ Representative
Promise...................... My Word
Nervous...................... Excited
Write It Up................. Fill in the Blanks
Place the Order.......... Secure Your _____
Learning..................... Mastering
Mistakes..................... Actions That Did Not Work
Errors .... Opportunities to Improve

Beyond these, certain words just send up red flags. Have you ever heard someone say "You *never* gave me that material you promised?" *Never* is a long time for what is probably a very short-term transaction. Other words can send up red flags; notice and avoid them. Be conscious of the words you use and how they might impact the people with whom you are trying to speak. Also, be aware of words that impact you negatively and figure that they must have a similar impact on others.

What Now?

Because positive and confident communicators are not born but made, you will want to continually practice the strategies described in this chapter.

Toolbox Tips

- Remember, only six percent of communication is about the words we use; the rest is nonverbal.
- Observe constantly; you cannot control anything you cannot see, hear, or feel.
- Be aware of the outcome you want. If what you were going to say helps achieve it, great. If not, don't say it.
- Practice listening more than talking.
- Take yourself out of the picture, and look at things from the other person's perspective. You'll stand a better chance of getting what you want if you can make it about the other person.
- Watch your language. Some words work, while others don't.

APPENDIX I

Worksheets

WORKSHEET 1: MY TOOLBOX

Use this worksheet any time you are confronting a new problem or situation.

Issue/Situation:_____

Desired outcomes:

1. _____
2. _____
3. _____
4. _____
5. _____

Feared outcomes:

1. _____
2. _____
3. _____
4. _____
5. _____

Tools I know I have:

1. _____
2. _____
3. _____
4. _____
5. _____

Tools I wish I had:

1. _____
2. _____
3. _____
4. _____
5. _____

Tools I have seen others use effectively in similar situations:

1. _____
2. _____
3. _____
4. _____
5. _____

WORKSHEET 2: MY PROFESSIONAL SILO

Imagine yourself as head of your own group. Write it down right now:

The _____ **Group**

[your last name]

From now on, every time you meet someone and get his or her business card, add a copy of it to this worksheet. You may want to leave space to the right to make notes. Each contact is a specialist consultant in your group.

WORKSHEET 3: MY 8 KEYS TO A COMPETITIVE EDGE

Eight strategic practices make a difference between getting what you want and being stuck with what you get. Take out this assessment periodically and see how you are doing:

		Getting It!	Stuck in Neutral	Need Help	In Reverse
Mind Game Strategies	Control Negative Self-Talk	☐	☐	☐	☐
	Find Peak Performance Zone	☐	☐	☐	☐
	Prepare for Competition	☐	☐	☐	☐
	Develop Rapid Recovery	☐	☐	☐	☐
Business Performance Strategies	Employ Power Communication	☐	☐	☐	☐
	Network Strategically	☐	☐	☐	☐
	Influence with Integrity	☐	☐	☐	☐
	Plan Strategically— Short and Long Term	☐	☐	☐	☐

The strategy I use most consistently is:

_____

_____

_____

_____

The strategy that would be most helpful to me in meeting my current professional goals is:

_____

_____

_____

_____

The strategy that would be most helpful to me in meeting my current personal goals is:

_____

_____

_____

_____

The strategy I would most like to improve in over the next six months is:

_____

_____

_____

_____

Every day in every way I get better and better and better.

_____

_____

_____

_____

WORKSHEET 4: MY WISH LIST

Professional athletes use this list to focus and get to the top of their games. What would you like to happen in your life?

- ☐ Increase concentration
- ☐ Notice and control self-talk
- ☐ Manage and control stress
- ☐ Identify and control distraction
- ☐ Catch distractions earlier
- ☐ Enhance communications—interpersonal and media
- ☐ Control anger and aggression
- ☐ Increase energy
- ☐ Increase motivation
- ☐ Develop a strong vision for the future
- ☐ Control discomfort
- ☐ Improve personal performance
- ☐ Improve self-esteem and self-confidence
- ☐ Develop a personal strategic plan
- ☐ Identify and resolve subconscious blocks
- ☐ Identify and overcome obstacles quickly
- ☐ Improve business results
- ☐ Harness the power of your imagination
- ☐ Achieve success through persistence

WORKSHEET 5: MY SUCCESS

This book—and the strategies it contains—are intended to help you get exactly the success you want from life. Take a moment and visualize it.

☐ The changes I would like to make have already happened.

☐ I have programmed myself for the success I want.

☐ What would my life look like?

_____

_____

_____

_____

_____

☐ What would my life feel like?

_____

_____

_____

_____

_____

☐ What would my life sound like?

_____

_____

_____

_____

_____

WORKSHEET 6: MY SELF-TALK SURVEY

Use this worksheet to figure out how that little (or maybe not-so-little) voice in your head prevents you from achieving what you want—or need—to accomplish (and can truly contaminate your performance).

1. What are you saying to yourself? _____

    _____

2. When does it start? _____

    _____

3. What does it start? _____

    _____

4. Who's there? _____

    _____

5. What going on? _____

    _____

6. Where, what's the location? _____

    _____

7. When is this happening? _____

    _____

8. Time of day? Day of the week? _____

    _____

9. How long does the self-talk last?_____

_____

_____

10. How loud is it? _____

_____

_____

11. When does it end? _____

_____

_____

12. How does it stop? _____

_____

_____

13. Do you have a way to stop it? _____

_____

_____

14. Does it just fade out? _____

_____

_____

15. Is it always your voice? _____

_____

_____

16. If not, whose? _____

_____

_____

WORKSHEET 7:
MY PEAK PERFORMANCE ZONE SURVEY

Close your eyes just for a moment. Now imagine yourself performing at your absolute peak whether on stage, on the field,
or in the boardroom. Notice that your sense of reality is different from usual:

- A fast game may have slowed down.
- A round of golf may have gone very quickly.
- An entire room, auditorium, or stadium full
  of people may seem to disappear.

Recognize and enter your peak performance zone.

1. What do you hear? _____
   _____
   _____

2. What sounds disappear? _____
   _____
   _____

3. What do you see? _____
   _____
   _____

4. What happens to clarity?_____
   _____
   _____

5. What do you feel like inside? _____
   _____
   _____

6. What do you feel like outside? _____

_____

_____

7. What do you smell?_____

_____

_____

8. What happens to time? Does it speed up? Does it slow down?

_____

_____

9. What happens to your speed? _____

_____

_____

10. What can you use to turn this on? _____

_____

_____

WORKSHEET 8: MY DISTRACTIONS INVENTORY

We are masters of creating distractions to prevent us from doing the work we have established as important. Kids, pets, email, the Internet, stock market performance, and many other distractions can take our attention away from where it should be directed. Take a moment and list the top ten distractions in your life:

1. _____
   _____
   _____
   _____
   _____

2. _____
   _____
   _____
   _____
   _____

3. _____
   _____
   _____
   _____
   _____

4. _____
   _____
   _____
   _____
   _____

5. _____

6. _____

7. _____

8. _____

9. _____

10. _____

WORKSHEET 9: MY MAGIC WAND OF 20XX

"Someday" is never going to come. In order to achieve goals, you need to envision them done—and for that you need a specific date. The Magic Wand of 20XX helps you envision where you want to be in five years, outline the steps you need to take to get there, and keep your sights on the prize.

Five Years from Now: 20 ____

My personal life will include:

1. _____

_____

_____

2. _____

_____

_____

3. _____

_____

_____

4. _____

_____

_____

5. _____

_____

_____

My business life will include:

1. _____
   _____
   _____

2. _____
   _____
   _____

3. _____
   _____
   _____

4. _____
   _____
   _____

5. _____
   _____

My financial affairs will include:

1. _____
   _____
   _____

2. _____
   _____
   _____

3. _____
   _____
   _____

4. _____
   _____
   _____

5. _____
_____

These things will be part of my life:

1. _____
_____
_____

2. _____
_____
_____

3. _____
_____
_____

4. _____
_____
_____

5. _____
_____
_____

WORKSHEET 10: MY SUCCESS EQUATION

The formula for success can be boiled down to one simple equation:

Success = Persistence + Imagination

You need both parts. When you're stuck, try this:

1. Envision your goal.
    a. What does it look/feel/smell/taste/sound like?
    b. How will it feel when you get there?
    c. Can you see yourself enjoying having gotten there?
2. Anticipate the obstacles you are likely to face—and how you will overcome them (or simply wait them out):

Likely Obstacle	Strategy for Persisting

WORKSHEET 11:
MY ODR (OBSTACLES, DISTRACTIONS,
AND RESISTANCE)

When you're working on achieving a specific goal, you can often talk yourself out of it in some surprisingly indirect ways. Go back to your Magic Wand of 20XX and pick one of your goals.

What can you see getting in the way?

1. _____

_____

_____

2. _____

_____

_____

3. _____

_____

_____

4. _____

_____

_____

5. _____

_____

_____

6. _____

_____

_____

7. _____

_____

_____

8. _____

_____

9. _____

_____

10. _____

_____

11. _____

_____

12. _____

_____

13. _____

_____

14. _____

_____

15. _____

_____

16. _____

_____

17. _____

_____

What is going to help you achieve that goal? (List only things
that are reasonable and within your grasp today.)

1. _____

   _____

2. _____

   _____

3. _____

   _____

4. _____

   _____

5. _____

   _____

6. _____

   _____

7. _____

   _____

8. _____

   _____

9. _____

   _____

10. _____

   _____

WORKSHEET 12: MY TRUNK CARD

Use this worksheet when you need to devote all of your attention to something and need to postpone distractions until later.

The three things most likely to distract me from what I need to do right now:

1. _____
_____
_____

2. _____
_____
_____

3. _____
_____
_____

I promise myself I will avoid thinking about these things until:

Date: _____

Time: _____

Now put the card away somewhere. It's particularly effective to put it in a place you can close with a noise, such as a car trunk.

WORKSHEET 13: MY MENTAL SUCCESS DVD

Many people relive their failures over and over. We turn them over, looking at every angle, every outcome, every possibility. The result? We frequently expect to fail. Turn that around and do the same thing with your successes and you will have an incredibly powerful tool. Here's how:

Imagine the last time you really succeeded in the kind of situation that is still important to you now.

1. When and what was it? _____

    _____

    _____

2. How did it look/sound/smell/taste/feel? _____

    _____

    _____

3. Visualize where it took place: _____

    _____

    _____

4. Imagine the room from every conceivable angle:

    a. Where you were.
    b. Where each of the most important other players were.
    c. From above.
    d. From below.
    e. From behind you.

Go over the whole thing one more time. Now you have a mental success DVD you can play whenever you are about to face a high-stakes situation!

WORKSHEET 14: MY SKEPTICISM SCHEDULE

Skepticism is a useful tool for evaluating information, people, and situations. When you're in the middle of a process, though, it can really get in your way. Put it off until a time when you can reasonably focus on it, and you may find yourself zeroing in on your own intuition. Use this worksheet to keep a running list of what raises your level of skepticism and when you are going to return to it.

I'm skeptical about:	I will think about it		Done
	Day	Time	

WORKSHEET 15: MY SWOT ANALYSIS

A SWOT (Strengths-Weaknesses-Opportunities-Threats) Analysis is a classic tool for assessing where you are in a given business or professional situation. It is a useful starting point for any new or renewed venture.

Strengths:

1. What talents have taken you to where you are professionally?
    a. _____
    b. _____
    c. _____

2. What do you do really well?
    a. _____
    b. _____
    c. _____

Weaknesses:

1. In what areas do you need to develop or improve?
    a. _____
    b. _____
    c. _____

2. Where do you need assistance in order to maintain and assure your professional or personal growth?
    a. _____
    b. _____
    c. _____

3. How do you protect your future? (You dream the future and look backward, avoiding things that might get in the way or derail you.)

    a. _____

    b. _____

    c. _____

Opportunities:

1. What opportunities are open to you today that you are not taking advantage of, both in and out of the office, on and off the field?

    a. _____

    b. _____

    c. _____

2. Are you looking far enough into the future? (With every decision, many CEOs are looking five years out and working backward.) YES NO

3. Is your lifestyle a risk to your company, its image, or its future earnings potential? YES NO

4. Are you or your product/service commercial or endorsement material? YES NO

Threats:

1. What threats exist for your company right now?

    a. _____

    b. _____

    c. _____

2. Which are internal, and which are external?
    a. _____
    b. _____
    c. _____

3. What threats do you see emerging in the next five years?
    a. _____
    b. _____
    c. _____

Some possibilities include:

- Letting someone else control your company
- Asking the wrong people the wrong questions
- Not seeking second opinions
- Inaction

WORKSHEET 16: MY @#$% LIST

Use this worksheet with members of your team to identify potential issues your organization faces—everything we can do to screw up our business, lose customers, and decrease revenues:

1. _____

_____

_____

2. _____

_____

_____

3. _____

_____

_____

4. _____

_____

_____

5. _____

_____

_____

6. _____

_____

_____

7. _____

_____

_____

8. _____

_____

_____

9. _____

   _____

10. _____

    _____

11. _____

    _____

12. _____

    _____

13. _____

    _____

14. _____

    _____

15. _____

    _____

16. _____

    _____

17. _____

    _____

18. _____

    _____

19. _____

    _____

WORKSHEET 17: YOU, INC. RESOURCES

When you are the CEO of a company, you can't do everything yourself. When you realize you have questions and no one you can safely ask, it's time to assemble a team to support you. Here are some key areas to consider:

Questions I need to ask:

Business Questions:

1. _____
_____
_____

2. _____
_____
_____

3. _____
_____
_____

Financial Questions:

1. _____
_____
_____

2. _____
_____
_____

3. _____
_____
_____

Legal Questions:

1. _____
_____
_____

2. _____
_____
_____

3. _____
_____
_____

Interpersonal Questions:

1. _____
_____
_____

2. _____
_____
_____

3. _____
_____
_____

Based on this inventory, I need to look for:

- Financial advisor/CPA
  Special focus:_____
  Must have experience with: _____
  Likely referral source: _____
  Date by which to hire: _____

- Business/performance coach
  Special focus: _____
  Must have experience with: _____
  Likely referral source: _____
  Date by which to hire: _____

- Attorney
  Special focus: _____
  Must have experience with: _____
  Likely referral source: _____
  Date by which to hire: _____

WORKSHEET 18: MISTAKES

Mistakes are expensive. Therefore, the greatest value most professionals and business people offer is that they help their customers avoid costly mistakes. You might even say you're in the business of selling mistakes. Take a moment and list the top ten mistakes your clients made before they became your clients.

1. _____
_____
_____

2. _____
_____
_____

3. _____
_____
_____

4. _____
_____
_____

5. _____
_____
_____

6. _____
_____
_____

7. _____
_____
_____

8. _____

_____

_____

9. _____

_____

_____

10. _____

_____

_____

WORKSHEET 19: MY IDEAL BUSINESS CARD

Visualization is a powerful tool for getting what you want. Imagine for a moment that you are in your ideal professional position. What would your business card look like?

Organization Name

Your Name
Position Title

Email: yourname@company.com   **P:** 1-MYBIGDREAM
Web: www.company.com   **F:** 321-555-3210

Email: **P:**
Web: **F:**

WORKSHEET 20: MY COACHING CULTURE

Our biggest impediment to growth is the way we cut things off, assuming we have the answers when it's much better to have the questions. A coaching culture—whether you create it for yourself or for your organization—can go a long way towards fostering positive, goal-oriented activity.

Part I: The Critical Task
Every time you need your team to approach an important task, this can help both of you focus:

Task: _____

Now ask:

1. What is your strategy for this task?
2. Is there anything you can think of that would get in the way of your getting the outcome you want?
3. What do you need from me?

Part II: Ongoing Effort
Like anything else, creating a coaching culture doesn't come overnight. We tend to get distracted by so many things— including our own expectations or need to be in control of other people. So:

1. Cultivate effective listening. In important situations, ask yourself:
   a. How well am I listening?

    b. What barriers am I erecting to proper listening?

    c. Do I find myself answering before the other person is finished speaking?

2. Employ questions instead of answers:

    a. What should you ask right now?

    b. How can you keep your questions open-ended?

3. Engage team members in coming up with strategies and solutions:

    a. When you encounter an objection, ask open-ended questions until you get to the heart of it.

    b. Always get your team members to articulate what you don't want to have happen.

    c. Ask how an issue can be solved before you express your own approach.

4. Always know what three things you can provide to assure your team of success.

WORKSHEET 21:
MY INTEGRATED WORKING BACKWARD STRATEGY

In order for your Magic Wand of 20XX to work well for you, you'll need to combine some of the strategies we've used in one place. Use a separate worksheet for each area that's important to you. For example, if the amount of money you make is important, write that down; if what you wear is important, write that down.

Area: _____

The year is [five years from now]: _____

_____ will look like: _____

_____ will feel like: _____

_____ will sound like: _____

Obstacles I Encountered:	Strategies I Used for Dealing with Them:

Things I did to @#$% up along the way:

_____   _____

_____   _____

_____   _____

_____   _____

_____   _____

_____   _____

_____   _____

_____   _____

Successes I enjoyed along the way:

_____   _____

_____   _____

_____   _____

_____   _____

_____   _____

_____   _____

_____   _____

_____   _____

WORKSHEET 22: MY SENSE OF "STUCKNESS"

Getting out of that uncomfortable sense of being stuck starts with identifying where you are stuck. Read these statements and see what feels true to you.

- ☐ I find myself struggling with balancing my career and personal life.
- ☐ I am considering a transition. Does it have to be trying and difficult?
- ☐ I frequently feel "stuck" in patterns that slow down my progress.
- ☐ My desires are frustrated because I have an aversion to confrontations.
- ☐ I am afraid to fail. Fear of failure is impeding my progress and detracting from my quality of life.
- ☐ Important new growth and profitability initiatives are stalled because of confused or less-than-effective management personnel.
- ☐ Key management personnel seem "split into camps" because they cannot agree on critical policy issues.
- ☐ Top management personnel feel isolated and lacking in effective sounding boards.
- ☐ I would like to have a confidential sounding board to advise me on people, culture, issues, and the psychology of everyday corporate life.
- ☐ The perception is that top management is out of touch with staff personnel.
- ☐ We are doing everything we can think of, but nothing is happening.
- ☐ What worked before isn't working now.

☐ I am facing some difficult communications with partners or family members (my children in particular).

Other frequently occurring STUCK signs:

In Business:

☐ We're having trouble closing the big deals.

☐ Our senior team is not working well or consistently towards the same goals.

☐ Members of our senior team need help developing specific skill sets.

☐ We don't want to make the same expensive mistakes others in our industry—or on our career path—have made.

☐ I want to achieve work/life balance without sacrificing top performance.

☐ I simply need a confidential sounding board.

In Athletics:

☐ Coaches, managers—even team owners—may experience one of the following:

☐ You notice a drop-off in a particular player's performance.

☐ You feel a particular player is not living up to his or her potential.

☐ A player seems distracted or unfocused on or off the field.

☐ Team members are not working together effectively or consistently. (Athletes may avoid talking about this.)

Individual athletes may experience:

☐ You're having trouble concentrating.

☐ You feel you have more to give to your game but cannot access it.

☐ You find yourself in a slump.

☐ Balance has become a significant issue in your life.

☐ You have no one you can safely discuss these issues with.

WORKSHEET 23:
MY NONVERBAL COMMUNICATION HABITS

Only six percent of communication occurs because of the words we use; the rest comes from body language, tone, etc. When you're first trying to understand what messages you are really sending, it's important to observe yourself. Go and have a few conversations with different people, and use this worksheet to help you record your observations. If you don't like the characterizations I've used for each continuum, cross them out and write your own words. I've also left you space to track another element you notice in your own communication.

Conversation with: _____

Voice Tone							
Tenor:	Commanding	○	○	○	○	○	Imploring
Inflection:	Falling	○	○	○	○	○	Rising
Manner:	Fierce	○	○	○	○	○	Gentle
Affect:	Altered/Artificial	○	○	○	○	○	Natural
		○	○	○	○	○	

Body Language

Stance:	Aggressive	O	O	O	O	O	Submissive
Energy:	Tense	O	O	O	O	O	Relaxed
Limbs:	Clenched	O	O	O	O	O	Open
Expression:	Forceful	O	O	O	O	O	Approachable
		O	O	O	O	O	

Speech Patterns

Conviction:	Certain	O	O	O	O	O	Hedging
Speed:	Rapid	O	O	O	O	O	Ponderous
Engagement:	Declaring	O	O	O	O	O	Inquiring
Flow:	Easy	O	O	O	O	O	Halting
		O	O	O	O	O	

Eye Contact							
Duration:	Continuous	○	○	○	○	○	Seldom
Comfort:	Assured	○	○	○	○	○	Uneasy
Breaks:	Forced	○	○	○	○	○	Genuine
Gaze:	Piercing	○	○	○	○	○	Fluttering
		○	○	○	○	○	

Summary: If this person couldn't understand my words, he or she might think I was:

- ☐ Angry
- ☐ Annoyed
- ☐ Approachable
- ☐ Assured
- ☐ Content
- ☐ Delighted
- ☐ Depressed
- ☐ Difficult
- ☐ Excited
- ☐ Happy
- ☐ Sad
- ☐ Unconfident
- ☐ Upset
- ☐ Worried

APPENDIX II

Quick Table of Issues

QUICK TABLE OF ISSUES

Primary Audience	Primary Issue	Start With	Also Read
	Struggling for work/life balance	Chapter 5: Working Backward	Chapter 1: The Wish List
	Considering a transition	Chapter 5: Working Backward	Chapter 1: The Wish List
	Feeling stuck	Chapter 9: Why Stuck is Not the Worst Place to Be	Chapter 3: Eliminating Distractions
	Avoiding necessary confrontations	Chapter 10: Communication Strategies for Peak Performance	Chapter 8: Preparing to Meet the Competition Versus Winging It
	Fearing failure	Chapter 4: Imagining Success	Chapter 2: Controlling Self-Talk
	Feeling isolated at the top	Chapter 6: You, Inc.	Chapter 7: Your Competitive Edge
	Having trouble closing the big deals	Chapter 8: Preparing to Meet the Competition vs. Winging It	Chapter 10: Communication Strategies for Peak Performance
	Finding that senior team members do not have the same goals	Chapter 5: Working Backward	Chapter 8: Preparing to Meet the Competition Versus Winging It
Businesspeople	Noticing that senior team members need help developing specific skill sets	Chapter 7: Your Competitive Edge	Chapter 10: Communication Strategies for Peak Performance
	Worrying that you may be making expensive mistakes	Chapter 6: You, Inc.	Chapter 5: Working Backward

Primary Audience	Primary Issue	Start With	Also Read
Coaches	Noticing a drop-off in a player's performance	Chapter 4: Imagining Success	Chapter 2: Controlling Self-Talk
	Sensing that a player is not performing up to his or her potential	Chapter 7: Your Competitive Edge	Chapter 5: Working Backward
	Observing that a player seems distracted or unfocused—on or off the field	Chapter 3: Eliminating Distractions	Chapter 4: Imagining Success
	Perceiving that team members are not working together effectively or consistently	Chapter 5: Working Backward	Chapter 8: Preparing to Meet the Competition Versus Winging It
Athletes	Having trouble concentrating	Chapter 3: Eliminating Distractions	Chapter 4: Imagining Success
	Feeling unable to access the best you have to give to your game	Chapter 8: Preparing to Meet the Competition Versus Winging It	Chapter 2: Controlling Self-Talk
	Finding yourself in a slump	Chapter 7: Your Competitive Edge	Chapter 9: Why Stuck Is Not the Worst Place to Be
	Experiencing balance issues in your life	Chapter 1: The Wish List	Chapter 3: Eliminating Distractions

APPENDIX III

Additional Stories

A lot of books present various theories and techniques that *should* work. But do they? The proof is in the application. That's why I have peppered this book with real-life stories from the clients I have been fortunate to help as well as some people who were willing to talk to me. As it turns out, there are many more stories than could possibly fit in the narrative. Here are some of my favorites we were not able to weave into the text. I don't think of them as "extra"; I think of them as "extraordinary." I hope you agree.

Create Your Own Zone:
Hedge Fund Analyst/Trader

One client, a very successful hedge fund analyst and trader, is constantly beset by distractions in his fast-paced world. He created a way for him to avoid distractions he called "the Hole." The Hole is part physical (he works in a secluded location with the doors shut and no phones ringing). But it's also part mental; my client has to get himself in the right head space to enter the Hole. Here's what he wrote to me about four consecutive days in the Hole devoted to a particular strategic project:

> On day one I had complete clarity of thought and was incredibly productive. In spite of the long stretches of concentration, I felt energized. I was insightful, my brain was working at a high level, and I was able to build a mental model of what I was learning and a to-do list of what I still need to learn to complete the mosaic. I

finished wanting to do more and wondering why I don't do this all the time.

The second day I was in the Hole virtually all day, aside from one ninety-minute conference call. I was really aware that the faster I can recognize when I'm distracted, the faster I can get back in.

By day three there was this amazing feeling. I felt highly productive and ended the day feeling complete. I had this highly unusual sense of being able to relax at night.

On day four I found increased clarity of thought and, surprisingly, conviction. Conversely, when I am doing my usual thing, flitting from project to project, I'm like a waif in the wind. I also noticed that I was much less irritable when in the Hole than I tend to be outside of it.

In the Pool: John Repetti

John Repetti is a very successful CPA. In his business, he likes to use the 1,000-foot approach before pitching a business idea to a prospect. He has a team responsible for various details—right down to the granular level, and he synthesizes the information to deliver a winning message and convert the prospect to a long-term client.

The day before a meeting, John will reread all the material. He'll meet with his team of experts and discuss how they are going to approach the particular client. Each player has a specific role based on her or his respective strengths. Being less than prepared is simply unacceptable—and that includes showing up for the meeting late or even rushed. We figure that ten minutes early is barely on time.

"I always know who the decision makers are in advance. I strive for as much information about them as possible, including their goals and objectives as well as their emotional hot buttons," John says, "so in the meeting itself I can pay attention to the key players' body language. The meeting can dynamically change based upon body language and tonality, and my team and I need to be ready to adjust."

John knows a lot about preparation for competition. He was a champion springboard diver, with only himself to depend on. He explained how he got in the habit of preparing to dive: "My mindset had to be absolutely pristine. I couldn't think 'Don't balk.' All I could do was think about perfect execution. During practice I would get ready by looking for a 'spot' on the way into the water—a light on the ceiling, a branch on a tree, etc. During the competition I would have that spot as an extra weapon."

I asked John about the difference between preparing for a business meeting and springboard diving. "None," he said. "The dive is always the same, but the water is always different. True competitors get 'in character' and plan their approach to whatever pool they are diving into."

A Record Mindset: Craig Pinto

Professional indoor football player Craig Pinto, a kicker with the New Jersey Revolution, says his life changed when he was diagnosed with celiac disease. Through a lot of hard work, Craig conquered some of the disease's worst side effects—lethargy and weight gain—and went on to live his dream. But that wasn't quite enough for Craig; he started a charity—the Kicking for Celiac Foundation—to raise money for research and education.

Craig decided that one way to draw attention to the foundation—and to celiac and Crohn's diseases—was to break the world record for most field goals kicked in a twelve-hour period. Each attempt had to be made from at least forty yards. Craig figured he would try for 500 goals, which would set a new record that would be tough to beat.

By the time the day of the event ended, Craig had made 717 field goals. And you know what's most amazing? He *missed* the first kick. Most of us, upon making a mistake like that, would start to brood on it, internalize it, and let it interfere with our whole set of goals. Not Craig.

"I kind of chuckled at that first miss and thought, 'Well, this could be the start of a day full of misses, but I have twelve hours to find out, so I may as well make the best of it and shake that off,'" he says. Although he figured it would take until late afternoon to reach his goal, Craig actually accomplished it at one forty-five. "As the rest of the day progressed, I kicked for about an hour on, then half an hour or so off. I wanted to make sure I set the bar high for anyone who might attempt to break the record in the future. Also, once I had achieved my goal, I wanted to exceed it."

How do you get ready to kick a football for twelve hours straight? Craig says his preparation was ninety percent mental and ten percent physical. "I've kicked footballs for sixteen years—in high school, college, and the AIFA. I knew that I knew how to kick. I needed to prepare my mind. So while I would practice and do exercises to build up leg endurance, I really focused on my head. I practiced focusing on the entirety of the scenario so that I could kind of take myself out of my body and look down on the event."

"I also focused on *after* the event—what it would be like having achieved this record I would be eternally proud of. I locked it into my mind that I would set a world record and be part of *The Guinness Book of World Records*, which I liked to read when I was a child. I repeated that in my mind and tried to feel the aftereffect and the joy that came with it. If anyone raised any doubts that it was possible, I deflected them, because in my mind I knew I would do it. Failing was not an option—or even a thought in my mind."

Aside from a world record, what did Craig get from his experience? "For future endeavors, I think this will give me a different bit of strength I may not have had before. In instances where I may be tested physically, I know I can put myself through physical discomfort for a good cause and create a positive outcome. More important, I know I can potentially put my mind to anything, and achieve it."

Play It Again: Jourdan Urbach

Concert violinist Jourdan Urbach understands the risks of getting out of the zone:

> As a performer, it's incredibly important to remain in your Peak Performance Zone. When you're out of the zone, your performance can get too mechanical. You fall into "autopilot." You blow through the most difficult lines and

runs without any consideration for adding your own artistry to the piece. When that happens, the performance falls flat.

For me, it can sometimes be easy to get distracted from my zone. Negative thoughts about schoolwork, stress about multiple engagements, concern about preparation—all of these things can drag me out of the place where I need to be.

The way I *Click!* back into my zone before a performance is to play the first line of the piece over and over, mastering it and making it mine. This way I know for sure I will start off on the right foot and will enter my zone from the very beginning.

Being in the zone is the point where my bow feels more like an extension of my arm, my fingering becomes intuitive, and everything draws from my center, from within, in a Zen-like way.

Back on Target: Charlie Blankstein

Charlie Blankstein is a competitive shooter. When he first came to work with me, he was finding that bad performance on one station could destroy his concentration for the rest of the course. We helped him develop a *Click!* to clear his mind and refocus. Here's what he has to say:

As a competitive shooter, it's easy to get off track when you have a bad station or two.

When it happens, you focus on the two bad stations instead of the fourteen you have ahead of you. You spend more time thinking *How could I have missed that shot?* instead of *Oh well, I'll get the next one.*

But when I began working on my concentration, improving my self-talk, thinking about my Click!, I began to improve dramatically. I began to think positively about the upcoming target instead of negatively about targets missed. I would visualize the next station as a successful one. These days, I perform at a far higher level.

The Roar of the Crowd: Ken Davidoff

Imagine having to write 600 words in twenty minutes while in the middle of thousands of screaming people. Ken, a baseball writer for *Newsday* and a commentator for ESPN, has to complete a tight story that captures all the action—and to do it while the action is winding up.

Unlike a lot of people I know, Ken has found a way to feed off the chaos of his work environment, and it helps him write. He finds he cannot zone out while he's writing because he has to keep aware of the sounds around him. He splits his mind into two tracks, one focusing on writing and the other keeping an eye and ear on what's going on around him.

Ken tells a story about an author who had written books and wanted to try his hand as a baseball journalist. He could not handle the pressure of writing on deadline. Ken finds that repetition is important. If you make the deadline once, you can make it again; if you manage to create two sharply focused tracks in your mind for one game, you can do it for another. Ken also advises that it helps to start young.

Feeling Is Not Fact: Alice Spitz, Esq. and Sal DeSantis, Esq.

Alice Spitz and Sal DeSantis, personal injury attorneys with Molod, Spitz & DeSantis in New York City, thrive on pressure. Their performance can make or break cases for their clients. Sometimes millions of dollars—or the possibility of rebuilding a shattered life—are at stake. So they prepare—and they trust their preparation.

During a trial, Sal is particularly careful not to let negative thoughts interfere with his carefully worked-out game plan. The opposing attorney may say things to throw him off base. The trick is to listen enough to adjust his evidence and responses to match those of the other side without letting the other side get into his head and spook him. Sal knows he is in his zone when he finds that time is going really fast (when things are not going well, time seems to drag). He spoke to me about one summation when he had an almost out-of-body experience.

"If you had asked me to memorize a poem, I couldn't have done it, but I was able to talk about medicine, create little vignettes for the jury, and be persuasive. I have to tell you I was afraid and could virtually see myself sweat, but I kept on, trying to brush aside any negative thoughts I was having. One juror told me later that I had put it together for them even though I wasn't sure it had gone so well."

Alice has a similar story. "Once I had to do a deposition

with a horrible head cold. It took the full day. I was sure the transcript would come back a mess, but it was just fine. Even though I wasn't feeling my best, my preparation paid off."

I spent a lot of time talking with Alice and Sal about juries. Of course, there is a lot of science behind jury selection and there are now jury consultants (I do this for some clients), but most experienced litigators develop an instinctual approach. This often results in talking to specific jurors.

"During the most difficult trial of my career, I had what I thought was an indifferent—if not hostile—jury," Alice recalls. "But two jurors in the front row seemed to be with me the whole time. I started to feel these were the people I was talking to. After I won the case, I told one of the 'with-me' jurors how I felt her support. She told me they had been leaning towards me just to admire my manicure! Still, my ability to change my focus from worry to rallying the troops won the day for my client."

What do we learn from these anecdotes? That feeling is not fact. Alice and Sal trusted their preparation, refused to listen to negative self-talk, and kept taking the next best step—working through the situations to the end goal rather than derailing themselves with worry.

All the World's a Stage: J. Robert Spenser

If there is one place where performance is critical, it's the theater. Turn in a lousy, indifferent, or uninspired performance and your current role might be your last. J. Robert Spenser is a seasoned Broadway actor who has appeared in award-winning shows including *Jersey Boys* and *Next to Normal*.

He told me how he struggled with getting into the zone

and shared what works for him now. "Before any performance of *Jersey Boys*, I would do all the typical relaxation exercises that most stage actors do. I'd listen to the standard calming music and do some stretches. But I slowly discovered that doing more-abstract things worked better for me.

"Lately, in *Next to Normal*, I've been painting before performances. I also sometimes play the guitar. Through these forms of expression I'm focused in a way different from anything I've experienced before."

Everyone finds a different approach to getting in the zone. If you try something and it doesn't work, try something else. Go to wherever you feel engaged but calmly energized and in control.

Finding Your Motivation: Rohan Murphy

You may not have heard of Rohan Murphy, but you have certainly seen him. Rohan lost his legs at birth, but that didn't stop him from having a successful career as a wrestler, both in high school and at Penn State. He also became an accomplished powerlifter, representing the United States at competitions all over the world. He has been featured on ABC News and in *Sports Illustrated*, and he did a commercial for Nike. Rohan, now a motivational speaker, knows the power of the mind game in everyday life:

> The first thirteen years of my life I wanted to be out there with all the other kids playing little league baseball and travel soccer. Unfortunately, because of my disability I wasn't able

to play all the sports my friends were playing. Then I found the sport of wrestling, and I stuck to it like glue.

Going through something unique like I did gives you a different perspective on life. When it comes to competing in sports, I have always thought the key was motivation. What's motivating that athlete to be out there? Is it the money, scholarship, love of the game, or a parent? Is it extrinsic or intrinsic motivation?

I think most younger athletes are intrinsically motivated; they have a passion for whatever sport they are playing. But as athletes get older and realize what benefits they can obtain from being good at a sport, that's when the extrinsic motivation comes in! Maybe it's the pressure of getting a college scholarship or trying to get a new max contract next season as a professional. I really believe athletes nowadays are more extrinsically motivated than ever!

Who can blame them? Everywhere they go their favorite athletes are trying to sell something on the Internet and television and in magazines. Everyone wants to be the poster boy for some company like Nike or Gatorade. Is it their fault, or is it society's fault?

Regardless, intrinsic motivation still plays an essential role. I know when I compete, I'm intrinsically motivated to be the best athlete I can be! I appreciate being out there on the playing field. I don't take that for granted! It's probably because I know what it feels like not being able to compete in sports.

Every Game Is a Mind Game: Anthony Becht

Versatile NFL player Anthony Becht played 152 consecutive games from 2000 to 2009, placing after only Brett Favre and Peyton Manning among offensive players. Anthony was injured many times but found that mental toughness and focus allowed him to channel through the pain and play at a high level.

I first met Anthony at a party at Mickey Mantle's. He was skeptical of the idea of a sports strategist until I showed him it was all about getting an edge—however slight. Here's what Anthony had to say about our work together:

> When you're on the playing field, everything is going a million miles an hour. You need to slow it down and tighten the focus so nothing but the ball matters. Staying at the top of your game really comes down to the mental edge— in all sports and in all positions. If you make a mistake on the field, you have to be able to bounce back. Before you even get there, you have to home in on your priorities and opportunities and clear away the rest of the week. The techniques Doc Schaefer offers are outstanding for doing this. I have used them in a variety of situations—on and off the field—to be more productive and mentally prepared.

Building Up the Jones Group: The Secret Core of You, Inc.

In Chapter 6 I talked a lot about how every person who wants to be successful needs to see himself or herself as the CEO of a company. A key part of the You, Inc. approach is assembling teams of experts you can call upon for any reason. How do you do this?

Some very innovative people I know have started networking groups. These groups throw a massive number of tools in your toolbox almost instantly. Here are seven groups from which I or my clients have derived benefit. Everyone concerned about performance should have at least two such groups in her or his toolbox.

- Fred Klein and Nancy Schess are partners in a law firm. They created Gotham Networking (www.gothamnetworking.com), which has evolved into a community of nearly 600 members. Participants in Gotham agree with two core maxims: "It is better to give than to receive" and "What goes around comes around." Gotham has a strong cohesion that is almost familial or tribal, and members function as noncommissioned salespeople for each other.

- Ellen Volpe and Gene Brown run American Business Associates (www.aba-ny.com), a group that specializes in strategic networking. Ellen, Gene, and Bob Putt, who runs the New Jersey Council of ABA, hold weekly meetings that create an environment that allow people to get referrals while enhancing their business skills. They subscribe to a strategic networking approach, where bringing people together as resources for each other and for their clients is better than just looking for leads.

- After a bout with cancer in 1987, financial advisor Bernie Ascher decided to look for ways to bring more value to his clients. With a strong family orientation and a passion for the simple joys of life, Bernie understood the importance of relationships. In seeking to help his clients achieve more than financial goals, he invented Navigators (www. navigatorsgroup.net). The group consists of carefully screened—and well-connected— experts in a wide range of fields. When a client of one Navigator is having an issue— or wants to achieve something—the other Navigators serve as a sounding board, and one can typically provide additional help.

- Sales trainer Adrian Miller found that she was having trouble getting her clients to go to networking groups because of the time involved and the inconsistency of results. So she formed Adrian's Network (www. adriansnetwork.com) on a unique call-in model. Calls occur several days a week at different times of day. Participation on each call is limited so that everyone gets a chance to speak. Adrian also actively makes introductions when she thinks members can be helpful to each other.

- Banker Steve Krauser was frustrated with networking efforts that led to a stack of business cards but no business. His group, Network Associates, focuses on the concept that the importance of networking is not to count the people you meet but to meet the people who count. He builds relationships with people who can be resources for his clients. He avoids doubling up on resources, insisting that each individual be able to bring something different to the table and be able to help his clients.

- Health and benefits expert Jeff Weiner hosts a roundtable lunch group. At each lunch 10 of his 400-plus contacts get together to discuss issues. Jeff carefully selects attendees for each group.

- Risk management expert Ron Tucker created the invitation-only Tucker Group (www.rontuckergroup.com) to bring together experts in various fields. The group's motto is "an informal networking group focused on helping each other do more business." Discussions at each meeting center on a variety of business issues, and members are encouraged to make referrals to each other only if it makes perfect sense for their clients.

- Internet marketing authority and author

Jerry Allocca runs a networking group called LeadPro (www.leadpro-li.com/leadpro/default.htm), which focuses on developing the value of a business network over the long term because successful transactions are the result of solid relationships.

Testimonials for Dr. Dan Schaefer and the *Click!* System

The techniques in this book have been put to the test in real life by a wide range of people. Athletes at every level, performers, entrepreneurs, and top-level executives have worked with me to improve their performance. They may have attended one of my seminars, engaged me as a performance coach, or used me as a Confidential Sounding Board. Some of them have given me permission to share their thoughts with you—even though in some instances they wish to remain anonymous.

See you soon, Doc. I'm very excited to get started again and continuing a very successful college career. The *Click!* system has worked wonders for me both on and off the ice. By using the *Click!* strategy, my game was taken to a higher level almost immediately. Physically I feel better, and mentally I am noticeably a more confident and consistent performer. Between my training, experience, and drive, the tools for success have always been there for me. The *Click!* strategy helps me put the pieces together and realize my full potential, letting my subconscious respond and ultimately take over on the ice. The hardest part is stepping aside and allowing it to.

—A competitive athlete

When I met Dr. Dan, I was about to begin a new venture, teaching an adult education class in broadcasting (the very next day). I was apprehensive about how I would perform in this new role as I was already juggling my work in radio and my freelance work, including at News 12. During our brief conversation you reminded me about the value of my past failures and successes, how those experiences and lessons can help one be relaxed, alert, and in the moment, and how such a state of mind *will* lead to a successful performance. As I said, you were exactly the person I needed to be with! I think this epiphany can be distilled to: Dr. Dan helped me tap the lessons of my past to build confidence today about success in the future.

—David North, broadcaster and president,
David North Media

I was entering into the final negotiations for the sale of my 1B global company. The environment had become very conflicted. On the advice of my CEO I flew from Australia to New York and spent three days with Dr. Dan. When I walked into my key meeting I was prepared in a way that I never expected. The outcome was a major win, and I knew I had someone watching my back.

—J.P., Australia

As a senior financial executive responsible for the part of a global company's financial operation in Europe, I was in the middle of a very important merger. For me and the other execs Dr. Schaefer was coaching, the future was uncertain. Would I or my counterpart win this position? In addition, I had people within my own company who were after my position. Anticipating a key meeting knowing I was pregnant and soon to be on maternity leave, I was a bit nervous. But Dr. Dan designed a strategy that allowed me to win my position, increase my value to the company, oversee my European responsibilities, support my team, and enjoy my maternity leave. Although the strategy defied conventional wisdom, I must admit it proved extremely effective.

—R.D., France

I used Dr. Dan to improve my golf game as a way to access and validate what I had heard about his Confidential Sounding Board. It enabled me to publicly meet with him. In reality, I was approaching a major merger and wanted a strategist at my back. I am really good at what I do, but having someone with a 1,000-foot view along with strategies for persuasion and influence over a six-month period enabled me to achieve my desired outcome. Keeping this "under the radar" proved to be critical.

—R.B., New Jersey

I attended Dan Schaefer's "Golf and the Mind Game" seminar with much skepticism. How could I lower my handicap without ever picking up a club? The very next golf season, my handicap index came down from 18.6 to 17.1! The best part is that I haven't been consciously using all of the techniques Dan presented that evening. The benefits of the presentation do not stop there, because golf is just a cover for business. Applying Dan's golf techniques to my business has improved my focus and results.

—Michael R. Breitman, CEO, Action COACH

Dr. Schaefer and his approach have brought my golf game back to a level I didn't think I was going to revisit again. With his emphasis on focused attention, I have truly learned how to stay in the moment better than ever before. Similarly, his skill utilization of focus and peripheral attention has helped bring back my greatest weapon: my putting. Not only I am making putts again, but my feel is back, and most important so are those three-footers. I have done a great deal of work in this field in the past, and Doc's approach makes a lot of sense and is extremely useful in my game. I can't wait to have him work with some of my students next year.

—Jim Weiss, head golf professional,
Cold Spring Country Club;
former course record holder at Bethpage Black (65)

Traditionally, financial advisors like me are always trying to find the "bait" that might separate them from the rest. As you know, "It ain't easy." No matter where you lead the horse, you can't make it drink. However, "Taking the mountain to Mohammed" never hurts either. So I tried Dr. Dan's "Golf and the Mind Game" seminar. The bottom line is that Dr. Dan can pack a room! The attendance to his seminar was refreshing. Everybody wants to improve his or her golf game even if it means a sales pitch! The rest was up to me and my hard follow-up, and that was pretty encouraging too! Dr. Dan is a real find. You should integrate his talents with your own. Your clients will benefit on and off the golf course.

—Robert T. Bonagura, CFP®, CRPS®, financial advisor

Dr. Dan presented to our team in January 2009. The girls were absorbed by his presentation, a combination of practical methods to develop and maintain a mental edge and a Q&A session to address specific concerns. The team emerged from the session with a new focus and a cohesiveness that enabled them to sweep through their bracket of the playoffs. The most notable change was in our goaltender, who finished her career playing at a higher level than she had previously achieved. This culminated in a shutout of our crosstown rivals, who had previously defeated us three times that season.

—Jeff Schneider, coach,
Princeton High School Girls' Ice Hockey Team

ABOUT THE AUTHOR

Dan Schaefer, PhD, has studied the practical implications of the mind and its workings for more than thirty years. Dan leverages the knowledge he has acquired to help professional and collegiate athletes, entertainers, and top-level executives achieve a competitive edge and consistently perform at their best.

He works both to boost an individual's performance and to enhance the ability of teams to work together towards common ends. Some of his clients are well-known public personalities, international companies, and public agencies; others are independent businesspeople. Regardless, Dan offers each of them the same degree of insight and speed-dial service and the promise that he will be their Confidential Sounding Board.

Dan is a sought-after public speaker on performance issues and the competitive edge. He has been a guest faculty member at the College of Physicians and Surgeons of Columbia University and the graduate schools of New York, Adelphi, Hofstra and Rutgers universities. His popular Golf and the Mind Game seminar has helped hundreds of people shave strokes off their golf games—and apply similar strategies to their business lives.

Dan's previous book, *How Do We Tell the Children?*, coauthored with journalist Christine Lyons, provides adults with strategies to assist children with grief and trauma. The book has enjoyed multiple editions.

A native of Brooklyn, Dan currently resides in Roslyn, NY.

Find Dan online at www.peakperformancestrategies.com, www.confidentialsoundingboard.com, and www.golfandthemindgame.com.

There's $$$$ in Mistakes

How many times have clients come to you with problems that have cost them time, money, and aggravation that you could have spared them if only they had come to you sooner?

What would you say if I told you that you can use others' mistakes to:

- Build business
- Save clients a fortune
- Quickly separate yourself from the competition
- Tap into the invisible dynamic that causes people to make decisions

There's $$$$ in Mistakes will show you how to get more business and how to increase customer loyalty by doing openly what you already do under the radar. In this book you will see how dozens of professionals and businesspeople in a wide range of fields have gotten more of the business they wanted by altering their approach to selling.

Think of it this way: you can go into a complicated explanation of all the features of what you do. If you're more subtle, you can talk about the benefits. Most of the time, it's easier to attach a price tag than a value to either of those approaches.

How do you move out of the category of "cost center" or "business expense" and into the category of value-adder? What if you could say "I sell mistakes" and prove it with a few simple stories? Imagine how much more powerful your prospecting and networking conversations would be. The value is evident, the lines are clear, and everyone will want you on their side.

There's $$$$ in Mistakes also has profound implications for your interpersonal relations. What mistakes get made on a daily basis that screw up your relationships with family, friends, and colleagues? Figure out where you want those relationships to be—and what could get in the way—and you can avoid costly mistakes and create a more productive, satisfying life.

There's $$$$ in Mistakes provides a proven system tailored just for you. In this book you will read the stories and observations of a wide range of professionals and businesspeople. You'll learn how to anticipate mistakes before they happen. And you'll discover how to turn those mistakes into financial and interpersonal capital.

No matter whether you are paying the cost or enjoying the savings, *There's $$$$ in Mistakes.*